X.

D0009981

JAZZ
A CRASH
COURSE

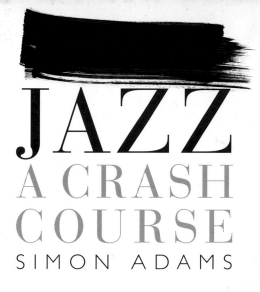

JAZZ
A CRASH
COURSE
SIMON ADAMS

WATSON-GUPTILL
PUBLICATIONS
New York

First published in the United States in 1999 by
Watson-Guptill Publications, a division of BPI
Communications, Inc., 1515 Broadway, New York,
NY 10036

Library of Congress Catalog Card Number: 98-89371

ISBN 0-8230-0979-3

*This book was conceived, designed,
and produced by*
THE IVY PRESS LIMITED
2/3 St Andrews Place
Lewes, East Sussex, BN7 1UP

Art Director: PETER BRIDGEWATER
Editorial Director: SOPHIE COLLINS
Designer: JANE LANAWAY
Editor: PETER NICKOL
DTP Designer: CHRIS LANAWAY
Picture Research: VANESSA FLETCHER
Illustrations: IVAN HISSEY

Reproduction and Printing in Hong Kong by
Hong Kong Graphic and Printing Ltd

1 2 3 4 5 6 7 8 9 10/06 05 04 03 02 01 00 99

DEDICATION

To Ann, with love and thanks

Contents

Introduction

Jazz—the soundtrack of the century, or just a load of noise? Art music for concert halls, or dance music for dives? From Lascaux to Jackson Pollock in 50 years, or not an art form at all? Whatever your take on jazz, this is the book for you. Not quite "everything you need to know about jazz," but it comes close.

Early jazz was played with fun in mind – song and dance, and often sex and booze as well.

This is a book of words and pictures, and jazz is all about sound. And over the course of this century—the lifespan of jazz—the sound of jazz has changed. From the classic melodies and rhythms of New Orleans through the massed ranks of swing to the torrents of bop and the raging fires of free jazz, the music has evolved and changed beyond all recognition. In trying to convey this constant flux, words are a poor substitute for the music itself, so listen to all and everything you can,

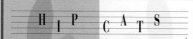

Hip Cats widens the scope, providing name checks in a selective list of other musicians either working with, contemporary to, or influenced by the main men and women. More names to show off with.

live or recorded. But don't just listen to the notes or the instruments or the tune. Listen to the inspiration of the musicians, for the key to jazz lies in improvisation.

No single word in jazz terminology is more misunderstood than improvisation. "Making it up" fails entirely to convey the meaning of this complex yet natural process. When jazz musicians improvise, they do so largely using an existing melody, harmony, or rhythm as a springboard. Some brave souls clear their minds of everything and improvise from a clean slate, but even they can't totally eradicate the reflexes of jazz from their memory. Individual musicians do it solo; entire groups do it collectively; and what results can be anything from a few bars of music to entire compositions. And because it was improvised, the same sequence of sounds

Cab Calloway, one of the jesters of jazz.

*will never be repeated. That is
why jazz is so special: each
improvisation is unique to that
performance.*

*Scary stuff, but exciting, too. As
exciting as all the different musicians—
the great, the good, the drugged, and the
drunk—you will encounter in this book.
Some of their music will bowl you over;
some of it will leave you
cold. But since they went
to the trouble to play it,
you owe it to them to understand a little of
what it is they are playing. After that,
you're on your own, and with so much jazz
in so many styles now easily available,
your journey will be sheer bliss. Enjoy!*

Simon Adams

SIMON ADAMS

Louis Armstrong:
improvisation started
with him.

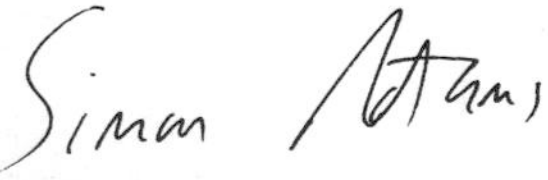

Timeline

Not so much a timeline,
because it's impossible
to run a continuous
chronology: jazz
musicians are constantly
tripping over each
others' solos, and their
styles collide, collude,
and interbreed with
each other. So more of a
contextual commentary,
a selected list of major
events happening at
the time the musicians
in question were
performing, to give their
music a social context
and to demonstrate how
all aspects of life are,
inevitably, fogbound in
the same Zeitgeist. It's
also a bit brainboggling
to discover that the first
jazz record is no older
than the Russian
Revolution.

How this course works

This course proceeds more or less
chronologically, although each
double-page spread is dedicated to
one musician, a group or connected

musicians, or a particular period or
style of jazz. And on each spread
there are regular features. It won't
take you long to work them out.

The instruments

There are few instruments known to humankind that have not turned up in jazz at some point. A handful, however, have defined the sound of jazz right from its origins.

Trumpet and cornet – Or rather, cornet and trumpet, since the main brass instrument used in early jazz was the cornet, smaller and squatter than the trumpet. By the time Louis Armstrong changed to trumpet in 1926, the two were virtually interchangeable and have been confused ever since. Along with the tenor sax, the trumpet is the sound of the jazz solo.

Trombone – Used in all the early jazz bands, the trombone was a big-band mainstay and gained a new life when free players from the 1960s onward explored its solo potential.

Clarinet – The favored reed instrument of early New Orleans bands. Benny Goodman, Artie Shaw, and Woody Herman were all clarinet-playing big band leaders in the 1930s, but fewer musicians have used it since.

Saxophone – The tenor saxophone, now the dominant solo jazz instrument, made its appearance in jazz quite late, when Coleman Hawkins established its mastery during the late 1920s. The alto also appeared in the 1920s, played by Tommy Dorsey, Frankie Trumbauer, and Johnny Hodges. The soprano was first played by Sidney Bechet in the early 1920s, then largely disappeared until John Coltrane picked it up in 1960. The baritone saxophone was played by Harry Carney after he joined Ellington in 1927, and subsequently by Gerry Mulligan in the 1950s and John Surman in the 1970s.

Flute – Came into its own in the 1950s, and was much used after the 1960s in jazz-rock and folk-influenced jazz.

Piano – One of the longest-serving instruments in jazz, the piano is used either as a rhythm instrument or as a solo instrument in its own right. The electric piano appeared during the 1950s, and the Fender-Rhodes, launched in 1965, dominated the sound of jazz-rock during the next decade.

Double bass – The double bass has had a leading role in jazz from the start, first as a rhythm instrument, then from the mid-1950s onward as solo. It was initially played with a bow (arco), but from the 1920s on musicians plucked the strings (pizzicato). The electric bass guitar, which began life in R&B groups, has supplanted the double bass in jazz-rock and fusion music since the 1970s.

Guitar – Although individual musicians played acoustic guitar, either as a rhythm instrument or solo, its lack of volume meant that its role was restricted. From 1939 Charlie Christian used an amplified acoustic guitar, but the introduction of the solid-bodied electric guitar into jazz-rock in the late 1960s established the instrument as one of the major solo instruments of jazz.

Banjo – Much used in early blues and jazz as a rhythm instrument, the banjo was replaced by the guitar in the 1930s and soon fell out of use.

Violin – Joe Venuti, Stuff Smith, and later Stéphane Grappelli gave it a solo jazz voice; in the late 1930s Smith was among the first to amplify his instrument. All-electric violins made an appearance in 1970s jazz-rock, notably with Jean-Luc Ponty. In recent years, Billy Bang and Leroy Jenkins have re-established the acoustic violin.

Drums – The basic rhythm instrument of jazz, in use from its earliest days.

Vibraphone – Lionel Hampton was the first major vibraphone soloist, and the instrument has continued its popularity at the hands of Milt Jackson of the MJQ, Gary Burton, and others.

Ben Webster, the late-night voice of the tenor saxophone.

1860 Approximately 20,000 New England shoe workers strike and win higher wages.

1864 During the Sand Creek massacre of Cheyenne and Arapaho, the U.S. Cavalry attacks tribesmen awaiting surrender terms.

1874 A review of Monet's painting *Sunrise* (1872) in *Charivari* magazine uses the term "Impressionism" for the first time.

1860~1900

In the Beginning
The Origins of Jazz

Emancipation brought little relief to the former slaves.

In the beginning was ... well, in the beginning was Africa. From Africa came the slaves, the slaves became free, and within a few years they developed their own unique music called jazz. And lived happily ever after, since this is all a story. A nice story, but a story nonetheless, for every art form has its own creation myth, and the myth of jazz is that it came from Africa. Which would have been news to the people of the southern states of the U.S.—black and white—for what they enjoyed and performed was not one music soon to be called jazz, but abundant musics in great and wondrous variety.

In at the real beginning of jazz was poverty. Despite emancipation at the end of the Civil War in 1865, the former slaves remained poor, many of them tied to the landowners they had worked for as slaves. Most were only semiliterate and relied for their entertainment on homegrown music. Work and field songs to sing while cutting cotton or building railroads, hymns and spirituals to sing in the segregated churches and prayer meetings, minstrel songs to perform in tent shows and on the vaudeville circuit, improvised songs sung by solo musicians accompanied by a simple banjo or violin—all these and more were performed across the southern states.

Obviously, music itself was color-blind. Minstrel singers were originally white performers who blacked their faces the better to imitate and caricature black musicians, while the white rural poor sang folk songs brought from Europe and Cajun music unique to French-speaking Louisiana. In the churches, black preachers borrowed a practice used in Britain to overcome the

Out of Africa?
The one element of jazz that undoubtedly has African origins is rhythm. In the music of West Africa—whence originated the slaves—rhythm was pre-eminent. Over a solid rhythmic foundation, cross- and polyrhythms developed: rhythms, often in triplets, overlaid on each other and set slightly out of phase. Such complexity was more sophisticated rhythmically than anything heard in European concert halls. What Europe contributed was harmony, but the vocalized bending and slurring of notes common in jazz owes more to the spoken languages of West Africa, where pitch and intonation mean as much as vocabulary, than to formal Western harmonic structures. In jazz the "dirty" vocal tones of black work songs are heard more often than a choral singer's pure intonation.

1878 The first commercial telephone exchange opens in New Haven, Connecticut.

1894 The Edison laboratories apply for copyright for one of their first films, *Edison Kinetoscope Record of a Sneeze*.

1900 Puccini's opera *Tosca* premières in Rome.

Traveling musicians played banjos and guitars and whatever other instruments came to hand, including homemade ones if necessary.

many more people to play instruments than were able to join the marching bands common across the South since the 1830s. The increasing range of instrumentation meant that black music grew increasingly sophisticated, and by the turn of the century it was ready to give birth to a new form of music known as ragtime—but the story of jazz has still not begun.

Spasm Bands

Great name; anything to do with sex? Sounds likely, given the origins of the word jazz—of which you will learn shortly—but a spasm band was a small group performing on street corners playing the popular songs of the day on homemade instruments. A guitar or ukulele provided the chords, a washboard, tambourine, or boom-bam—a broom handle studded with rattling metal bottle-tops—the rhythm. Helluva din, helluva lot of fun.

problem of illiteracy in the congregation by speaking two or three lines that were then repeated back by the congregation in a technique known as "lining out." All very similar to the call-and-response interplay between soloist and responding voices heard in the black churches and in the cotton-field work gangs.

Initially, all this music was vocal, with very little accompaniment from any kind of instruments. However, the availability of cheap military instruments after demobilization following the Civil War allowed

Harvest time in the cotton fields: the back-breaking reality of life in the rural southern states of America.

1897 Grape Nuts cereal is launched in the U.S. by C. W. Post and promoted as a health food.

1903 Wilbur and Orville Wright make the first ever man-carrying flights; the longest flies at around 852 feet and lasts 59 seconds.

1907 Pablo Picasso and Georges Braque develop the Cubist style of painting: Picasso's *Les Demoiselles d'Avignon* is hung in New York's Museum of Modern Art.

1895~1915
Classical Aspirations
Ragtime

Famous tune time: Maple Leaf Rag, Mississippi Rag, The Entertainer. *You know the songs, can hum the tunes, and might even be able to name some composers, but is it jazz? Has jazz got started yet? Well, no, not yet. We've still got a few years to go, and ragtime is but a small tributary of jazz, not the big river itself. So what, you ask, is ragtime doing in a book on jazz? The answer: without ragtime, jazz would have sounded very different, and generations of pianists would have been at a loss.*

F our words sum up ragtime—aspiration, composition, dissemination, and copulation (as ever). Aspiration, because it was the product of a growing black middle class who owned and could play pianos and who sought to create a new American classical music. Composition, because, unlike jazz and blues, which are largely improvised (as in, made up on the spot), ragtime was written down in advance. Dissemination, because printed ragtime songs quickly reached a wide audience— *Maple Leaf Rag*, published in 1899, soon sold a million. And copulation, because

the music flourished in the bordellos of New Orleans and other major towns and cities in the South, and music always hits the spot better if sex is involved.

Given that incompatible mix of high aspiration and low origins—prudish America was none too keen on music to grunt and groan with—it's no wonder

Treemonisha

Scott Joplin was never happy with the faintly disreputable associations surrounding ragtime, and hoped to turn the style into America's first classical, indeed black classical, music. He wrote his first rag opera, *A Guest of Honor*, in 1903, but dedicated the next eight years to what he considered his masterpiece—*Treemonisha*. This tale of a black foundling girl educated by whites was published at Joplin's own expense in 1911, but did not receive its première until 1915, with one disastrous performance at the Lincoln Theatre, Harlem. Its failure broke his mental and physical health, and he died in the Manhattan State Hospital in April 1917. "Maybe 50 years after I am dead my music will be appreciated": in 1972 the first professional production of *Treemonisha* in Symphony Hall, Atlanta, was a resounding success. A subsequent, and well-posthumous, Pulitzer Prize for music seems scant recognition.

Scott Joplin, the undisputed master of ragtime.

1910 The Argentinian tango becomes popular in Britain.

1912 Suffragettes begin a shop-window smashing campaign in London's West End.

1914 The zip fastener is introduced by engineer Gideon Sundback.

H I P C A T S

Scott Joplin *(1868–1917)*, **James Scott** *(1886–1938)*, and **Joseph F. Lamb** *(1887–1960) are the three composers who most define ragtime. Joplin was professionally trained and lived in St. Louis, Scott was based in Kansas City, while Lamb, who was white, hailed from New Jersey. Their classic Missouri ragtime style was lyrical and performed on solo piano at relatively slow tempos. Later rags speeded up and were arranged for bands and orchestras to play.*

Baltimore-born **Eubie Blake** *(1883–1983) adapted and updated the idiom, speeding it up and giving it more joie de vivre. Blake continued to perform at jazz festivals well into his 90s.*

Irving Berlin *(1888–1989) popularized the idiom even if his works, notably* Alexander's Ragtime Band *(1911), are more accurately rag songs than ragtime. But who cares!*

Joshua Rifkin *(b. 1944) revived ragtime in the 1970s, on the back of a film,* The Sting *(1973). His performances came as a shock, for he played ragtime slowly, just as Joplin intended it.*

Claude Debussy *(1862–1918),* **Erik Satie** *(1866–1925), and* **Igor Stravinsky** *(1882–1971) all used ragtime in their work, Debussy in* Golliwog's Cakewalk *(1908) and later piano works, Satie in* Parade *(1917), Stravinsky in* The Soldier's Tale *(1918) and other pieces.*

Ragtime

"White music played black" is a common description of ragtime, for this style owed its origins as much to white forms such as the polka and the march as it did to black banjo music and work songs. But what distinguished ragtime from its predecessors and gave it its distinct flavor was syncopation in the right-hand melody—literally, "ragged time." Out of this mold, Joplin created magic.

ragtime had a short life. While Scott Joplin devoted himself to writing ragtime operas, ragtime quickly lost its way, subsumed on the one hand by Tin Pan Alley and the American popular song, and on the other by the low-down, even more good-time, jazz music. But to both it contributed a rhythmic bounce known as syncopation, without which 20th-century popular music would have been duller by far. It also launched the careers of the quintessential American songwriter, Irving Berlin, and the masters of jazz piano, from James P. Johnson and Fats Waller to Art Tatum and beyond. Some legacy.

Fats Waller: the rhythmic legacy of ragtime lived on in his exuberant playing.

1900 Pneumatic tires are introduced by the Dunlop Rubber Company.

1901 The first transatlantic radio signal, the letter S, is sent in Morse code from Cornwall, England, and received in Newfoundland.

1903 Enrico Caruso makes his debut at the Metropolitan Opera in Verdi's *Rigoletto*.

1897~1917

Jazz Comes to Town

New Orleans Jazz

Jazz moves into New Orleans from the countryside.

More sex, please, we're musicians. Or rather, we musicians are in the part of New Orleans known as Storyville, named after Alderman Sidney Story, who in 1897 promoted legislation to confine prostitution to one part of town. Storyville was sufficiently well organized to have its own annual consumers' guide, The Blue Book, *which listed every working woman in the city. In each brothel, musicians played to entertain the clients and take care of business. Sex and jazz, at it like hammer and tongs, from the very beginning. Not that New Orleans was alone in inventing jazz—similar music was to be found across the rural South as well as in cities such as Baltimore and St. Louis. But let's keep it simple: too many facts get in the way of a good story.*

And in at the beginning was cornetist *Buddy* BOLDEN (1877–1931), about whom almost nothing is known. One photo, no recordings, but a mythical reputation that marks him out as the first named player of jazz. His band played a repertoire of popular dances, rough adaptations of ragtime, and the blues. Their six instruments reveal the mixed origins of jazz—cornet, valve trombone, and drums from the military brass bands, clarinet and double bass from the better-educated and richer mixed-race Creole community who lived in the city, and guitar from the traveling minstrels and blues singers. What it lacked in finesse, the band made up for in volume and earthy enthusiasm, for the music was played by ear, crudely improvised, and with little concern for pitch or intonation.

Basin Street, in the heart of New Orleans, a conglomeration of bars and brothels immortalized in an early jazz classic, *Basin Street Blues*.

1905 Pizza, a Neapolitan dish mainly eaten by the poorer classes, is introduced in the U.S., at Lombardi's in New York.

1913 Film censorship begins in Britain.

1916 Rasputin, the powerful and controversial Russian monk, is assassinated.

Jazz is the word

And the word, once again, is sex. Sorry to go on about it, but this time we're talking the Big O. Slang usage shortened orgasm to jasm or jass, which is how one of the first bands—the Original Dixieland Jass Band—spelled its name. Pranksters allegedly erased the J from their posters, so they changed the spelling to Jazz. Alternatively, we're talking an abbreviation for James; a French dialect verb *jaser*, to chatter; the adding of jasmine to perfumes (hence to jass it up); various African words; and musicians or dancers called Jasper or Jasbo. Take your pick.

Legion imitators took up where Bolden left off. Let's hear it for cornet players *Freddie KEPPARD* (1890–1933), *Bunk JOHNSON* (1889–1949), *Joe OLIVER* (1885–1938), and later *Louis ARMSTRONG* (1901–71), as well as clarinetist *Sidney BECHET* (1897–1959), and ragtime pianist *Jelly Roll MORTON* (1890–1941)—all began their careers in the bars and brothels in and around Storyville, playing a rough-and-tumble, boisterous music well suited to the cosmopolitan Crescent City. Many famous compositions take their names from the district—*Basin Street Blues* and *Canal Street Blues* the best known—and many of these musicians we will meet again later. By 1917, recognizable jazz music had taken shape.

At this stage, you'd probably like to listen to some early jazz. We know it was played collectively, with the cornetist taking the lead, a clarinet providing decoration, a trombone the punctuation, and guitar, bass, and drums the rhythm.

Doubling up the cornets, or introducing a saxophone for added color, were only permutations of a simple but winning formula. But unfortunately, the record industry had yet to register this new sound, and no recordings exist.

Marching bands—of variable quality but consistent enthusiam— are a feature of New Orleans life, especially at carnival time.

Buddy Bolden

The semimythical founder of jazz, Buddy Bolden was a laborer renowned for his inveterate womanizing, alcohol consumption, and his ability to play the cornet so loud he reportedly blew parts of his instrument off. We only know of his style through his protégé Bunk Johnson, who claimed to have worked with him (untrue, actually) and tried to reproduce his sound during the 1940s. But in forming a band with a brass and wind frontline and a string and percussion rhythm section, and in his use of melodic embellishment and improvisation, Bolden set a formula that was to serve as the basic template of jazz. Unfortunately for him, and for us, he smashed a pitcher on his mother-in-law's head in 1907 and was committed to the state asylum for the insane in Jackson, Louisiana, where he died unrecognized in 1931. Read all about him in *Coming through Slaughter* by Michael Ondaatje.

1917 Artist Marcel Duchamp shocks New York with his piece entitled "Fountain"— a white urinal signed "R Mutt."

1918 A flu epidemic kills an estimated 20 million people worldwide.

1918 Paul Robeson, singer, actor, and civil rights activist, graduates first in his class at Rutgers, Phi Beta Kappa.

1917~1920
Jazz Hits the Bigtime
The Original Dixieland Jazz Band

Dixieland

A lesson in semantics. To be strictly accurate, the term Dixieland should be applied only to white New Orleans groups, since Dixie was the name given to the eleven southern states that left the Union in 1861 rather than accept the abolition of slavery. In such circumstances, it is a tad offensive to describe original and inventive black groups as playing derivative Dixieland jazz. However, the term is often applied to New Orleans jazz as a whole—black and white—and in particular to its revival in the 1940s as Traditional or Trad jazz. Understood? Lesson over.

Introducing the band: leader Nick LaRocca on cornet, Larry Shields on clarinet, Eddie Edwards on trombone, Henry Ragas on piano, and Tony Spargo (born Antonio Sbarbaro) on drums. Ladies and gentlemen, a big hand for the first recorded jazz band in the world—the Original Dixieland Jass (soon to be Jazz) Band! Hurrah for the ODJB!

At last, jazz makes it onto record, the same year, 1917, as the U.S. enters the World War. But before you celebrate the triumph of black culture from New Orleans, two small wrenches must be thrown. The record wasn't made in New Orleans but New York, and the five ODJB members, despite being good New Orleans boys, were all white. So what's going on here, then?

Backtrack a year to 1916. Jazz had reached a critical mass, with white musicians getting in on the act and copying the styles of the original black groups. A number of record companies were sniffing around looking to record this new music, but they were in the cities of the North, while the musicians were mainly in the South. One man who was available, cornetist Freddie Keppard, working in Chicago and New York with the Original Creole Band, refused to record lest his work be plagiarized, thus passing up on the opportunity to be first into the history books. Thus it was pure circumstance that the band that got there first was a derivative group of white musicians.

The ODJB began life as Johnny Stein's Dixie Jass Band, five white men playing in the same frontline-and-rhythm-section format as established by Buddy Bolden.

Freddie Keppard, who could have been the first recorded jazz player, but wanted to keep his music to himself.

1919 Mexican rebel leader Emilio Zapata is ambushed and murdered by government forces.

1919 New Zealand-born physicist Ernest Rutherford discovers a way to split the atom.

1920 Actress Mary Pickford is prosecuted for bigamy following her marriage to Douglas Fairbanks.

In March 1916 they got a gig at Schiller's Café on East 31st Street, Chicago, and were reviewed favorably in the *Chicago Herald*. Despite their success, Stein was dumped as leader in June and the band was renamed. The following year, January 27, 1917, the band opened to a sensational reception in Reisenweber's Restaurant in Manhattan. After a trial session for Columbia Records, which declined to issue them, Victor Records snapped up the group and recorded two numbers on February 26. Thus, *Livery Stable Blues* and *Dixie Jazz Band One-step* were the first-ever jazz recordings and an immediate commercial success.

Say cheese. Matching smiles from the Original Dixieland Jazz Band.

The ODJB provided entertainment as much as jazz, imitating farmyard animals on *Livery Stable Blues* and introducing other novelties. Their performances were spirited, but stilted and primitive in comparison with what was soon to come. Derivative they might have been, and short-lived—they disbanded within a few years—but the ODJB earn their place in the history books for introducing jazz to a wider audience.

ALL THAT JAZZ

ORIGINAL DIXIELAND JAZZ BAND—*Livery Stable Blues, Dixie Jazz Band One-step* (1917), *Tiger Rag, Sensation Rag, Clarinet Marmalade Blues* (1918), *Jazz Me Blues, Royal Garden Blues* (1921)—collected on *Sensation* (ASV) and on *75th Anniversary* (RCA Bluebird).

Recording

Before the advent of electrical recordings in 1925, which used a microphone and electrical amplification, recording technology was a primitive affair. Musicians played into a large horn, which transmitted vibrations directly to a needle that cut a groove onto a wax cylinder or rotating disk. Copies of these were then made for sale. Quality varied wildly, with little dynamic contrast. Pianists therefore preferred to make piano rolls, which recorded a performance by perforating holes on a roll of paper. This was then played back on a piano-player or pianola. The clattering noise of the pianola, together with the ability of technicians to add extra notes to the piece by punching in more holes, favored the development of a fast, all-hands-on-the-keyboard style of ragtime. It is this sound, rather than the more measured classical approach of Scott Joplin, that defines ragtime for most people.

The pianola captured the ragtime sound.

1920 Rudyard Kipling is awarded £2 in damages from a medical firm which he has accused of using part of his poem "If" in an advertising campaign.

1921 The premières of two of Russian composer Sergei Prokofiev's most successful works take place in Chicago—Third Piano Concerto and the opera *Love for Three Oranges*.

1922 British Egyptologist Howard Carter discovers Tutankhamen's tomb in the Valley of the Kings.

1917~1925
Jazz on the Move
King Oliver

Goodbye, New Orleans! Hello, world! Or at least the major cities of the U.S. and western Europe. The recipe for this success was poverty and war, the method migration, as the trickle of black people fleeing Southern poverty and seeking jobs in the industrialized North became a flood. Jazz musicians moved with them, as the audience in the northern cities was bigger, and richer, and the clubs better. As it moved, jazz changed in style, losing its ragtime restrictions and taking on looser, more flowing rhythms.

France and jazz got along famously from the start.

The entry of the U.S. into the World War in 1917 led, after pressure from the Navy, to the closure of Storyville and the end of many music venues in New Orleans. Musicians' services were, however, required in Europe, where American troops were fighting on the Western Front. Jim Europe's Hellfighters Band, attached to the 369th U.S. Infantry, created a storm when it played in French cities in 1918, while the Original Dixieland Jazz Band enjoyed a nine-month postwar residency at the Hammersmith Palais in London.

HIP CATS

*The **Creole Jazz Band** contained, as well as Oliver and Armstrong, Honoré Dutrey on trombone, Dodds brothers Baby on drums and Johnny on clarinet, Bill Johnson on banjo, and pianist Lil Hardin, a rare and talented woman arranger and performer, and soon to be Louis Armstrong's wife.*

*Trombonist **Kid Ory** (1886–1973) led one of the most important New Orleans bands from 1912 to 1919, giving Louis Armstrong some invaluable early experience.*

*The **New Orleans Rhythm Kings**, with Paul Mares on trumpet and Leon Roppolo on clarinet, was the first white band to capture successfully the style and spirit of the black New Orleans bands, recording in 1922–25, with a revival in 1934.*

1922 The Cotton Club is founded in New York's Harlem.

1924 The German mark plummets. Adolf Hitler leads his "Beer Hall Putsch," marches on Munich with Goering and stormtroopers, and is arrested.

1925 Tennessee teacher John Thomas Scopes is convicted for teaching Darwin's theories of evolution to high-school students.

The black market

In 1920 the white recording industry woke up to the fact that out there was a black audience rich enough to afford gramophones to play jazz records on. In response to this surprising revelation, record companies began to issue Race Records—not the pejorative term it would be today—featuring black musicians and aimed exclusively at the black market. Independent labels such as Okeh and Vocalion made the running, but Victor and Columbia soon joined in, Columbia swallowing up Okeh in 1926. This racial divide lasted until World War II, although recordings by black artists seeped into general catalogs well before then.

The Creole Jazz Band, with King Oliver (seated) and Louis Armstrong (third from the right).

As one audience disappeared, a new, more widely dispersed one came on stream.

One man personifies this change. Cornetist *Joe "King" OLIVER* (1885–1938) moved north from New Orleans to Chicago in 1918, leading his own band on tour, and in 1922 beginning a residency at the Lincoln Gardens with his six-piece Creole Jazz Band. He sent south for a talented young cornetist, Louis Armstrong (see p. 22), to join him. The two transformed New Orleans jazz.

Until then, jazz had largely been an ensemble music, with improvisation confined to the odd bit of texture and detail. With two cornets in the frontline, King Oliver could experiment. While he kept close to the melody, Armstrong was let loose, elaborating in inventive and unexpected ways. Where once jazz had stomped along in steady time, now it began to ebb and flow, introducing tension into what had been an even-tempered music. It is our bad luck that Oliver didn't record until 1922, but don't ignore him, overshadowed as he is by his famous sideman, for his contribution was crucial.

The jazz aristocracy

King Oliver, Duke Ellington, Earl Hines, Count Basie, the Empress of the Blues, Lady Day—all very aristocratic for a democratic music from a republican country. But just as modern-day Americans are fascinated by all things royal, so early jazz fans accorded their heroes near regal status. At least Lester Young—the Pres—kept the American constitution alive.

1925 A working television is demonstrated by John Logie Baird.

1925 F. Scott Fitzgerald, chronicler of the "Jazz Age," publishes *The Great Gatsby*.

1925 Clarence Birdseye extends the scope of deep-freezing to precooked foods.

1925~1928

Hots Five and Seven

Louis Armstrong

Mississippi paddle steamer.

Enter the star, the innovator, the improviser, the man who turned jazz from pure entertainment into one of the major 20th-century art forms. Some achievement for the son of a New Orleans prostitute, deserted by his father at birth, born in a rough shack and brought up in poverty. A true rags-to-riches story, but few deserved it more than Louis ARMSTRONG (1901–71), because he had the vision to transform jazz, almost single-handedly. Breathless stuff, huh?

Armstrong invents

Until Louis Armstrong, improvisation in jazz was confined to brief, two-bar breaks. He developed the art of extended improvisation by taking a lengthy solo based on the harmonic structure—the chord sequence—of the song. After Armstrong, the ability to improvise, often at length, became the required skill of a jazz musician worth his salt, while jazz itself was to be dominated by the soloist in improvisatory flight.

A quick musical résumé: after early sponsorship by King Oliver, he begins career on the Mississippi riverboats in 1918, later that year replacing Oliver in Kid Ory's band. Relocates to Chicago at Oliver's behest in 1922. Urged on by his wife Lil Hardin, is hired by Fletcher Henderson (of whom more later) to work in New York in 1924. In 1925 returns to Chicago and forms own band—the Hot Five. History begins here.

With the Hot Five—Louis on cornet, then trumpet, Johnny St. Cyr on banjo, Johnny Dodds on clarinet, Kid Ory on trombone, and Lil Hardin on piano, later extended to a Hot Seven with John Thomas on trombone and Pete Briggs on bass—Louis broke the mold of New Orleans jazz. The collective style of performance gave way to a solo art, with the band in support of a star soloist. Technically brilliant,

"★"

"Pops"

A lovable man, a lovable nature, with a desire to be loved, reflected in the endearing nickname of Pops. Slightly less complimentary was "Satchmo," short for satchelmouth, such was the size of the regal gob that produced those beautiful notes.

Young Louis, already successful and with a life of stardom ahead.

1926 Elsa Schiaparelli begins her fashion career designing sweaters in Paris.

1927 *The Jazz Singer*, starring Al Jolson, opens in New York, marking the end of the era of the silent movie.

1928 Salvador Dali and Luis Buñuel collaborate on *Un Chien Andalou*, combining atomism techniques.

Louis Armstrong and his Hot Five in 1925, Louis swapping roles with wife/pianist Lil.

Cornet or trumpet?

The main brass instrument in early jazz was the cornet, a small, squat instrument used in the New Orleans marching bands. The transition from cornet to trumpet occurred with Armstrong, who switched instruments in 1926 because of the greater range and power the trumpet gave him. You won't be alone if you fail to distinguish the two, but as a rough guide, the cornet sounds more mellow, and can be played faster, than the harsher, brighter-sounding trumpet. Either can be played with a mute shoved into the bell to muffle the sound; then they sound almost identical.

ALL THAT JAZZ

LOUIS ARMSTRONG—*Louis Armstrong 1923–1931* (Jazz Classics in Digital Stereo): a good overview of his early work; *Hot Fives and Sevens* (JSP, two volumes): these famous tracks are essential for every jazz collection; *Louis Armstrong & His Orchestra 1928–1939* (Classics, nine volumes); *The California Concerts* (MCA, 4-CD set);1950s concerts with the All Stars. **BESSIE SMITH**—*The Empress* (Columbia): for an early glimpse of Armstrong's mastery, listen to his work accompanying blues singer Bessie Smith on *St. Louis Blues* and *Cold in Hand* (both 1925).

LATER ARMSTRONG

After 1928 Armstrong moved on. He starred in movies and after the war became a musical ambassador on tours organized by the State Department. His All Stars Band, formed in 1947, saw a return to small group work and cashed in on the New Orleans revival. By now he was a showman, a vaudevillian. Many found his clowning offensive, even racially unacceptable, as if conforming to a minstrel stereotype black musicians had grown out of. But Armstrong felt he had earned the fame, and money, and every so often a fine solo reminded his audience that this man personified the history of jazz.

endlessly inventive, utterly self-confident, and with considerable emotional depth, Louis's solos rewrote the jazz history books. Most famous is *West End Blues* (1928), with an opening flourish giving way to a melancholy theme that leads to an unbearably poignant final solo by Armstrong. *Potato Head Blues* (1927) and *Tight Like This* (1928) are no less grand.

1922 The British Broadcasting Corporation (BBC) is founded.

1923 The letters HOLLYWOODLAND appear on a hill above Los Angeles to advertise a property development.

1924 George Gershwin's "symphonic jazz" piece *Rhapsody in Blue* is enthusiastically received at its première in New York.

1920~1933
Onward, and Downward
The Jazz Age

Live and dance, while you may: a jazz poster from the 1920s.

Two things fueled jazz during the 1920s—alcohol, and the absence of alcohol. It might have been America's Jazz Age, when the world and its partner was dancing the Charleston and other new dances to the sound of a rapidly evolving jazz, but these dances were dry, since alcohol was prohibited in America in 1920. If you wanted a drink, you had to search for it. So paradoxically, as jazz hit the mainstream and became the music of the decade, it also followed drinking into the shadows, an accompaniment to illegal drinking, gambling, and other wholesome activities.

Jelly Roll Morton

Self-nominated creator of jazz, skilled ragtime pianist, composer, and arranger, a product of Storyville yet a commanding force in 1920s Chicago, Jelly Roll Morton (1890–1941) could have featured on every page of this book so far. The first important composer of jazz, he wrote many of his works, notably *King Porter Stomp* and *Jelly Roll Blues*, a decade or more before the first jazz recordings. With the Red Hot Peppers, which he formed in Chicago in 1926, he merged improvisation and composition into a meticulously arranged whole, producing an almost orchestral style way ahead of its time.

The effect of Prohibition—which came into force across the United States at midnight on January 16, 1920—was to drive drinking clubs underground, into the hands of mobsters and bootleggers. Those seeking a drink in one of the many speakeasies also sought music to accompany it, leading to a close association between the Mob and the jazz musicians who worked in the drinking dens. In retrospect, this aspect of the Jazz Age has probably been overemphasized, but the

1927 The fashionable Art Deco style is at its height.

1928 British actress Hermione Baddeley shocks society by wearing trousers at her wedding reception.

1930 Following an unsuccessful launch in 1928, sliced white bread finally goes on sale around the world.

association between drink, illegality, and jazz served to give the music a certain cachet that stood it in good stead, particularly with a young audience.

What that increasingly vast, multiracial audience heard was, at first, New Orleans jazz moved upriver and overland to Chicago. But as the decade wore on and jazz branched out across the country, new styles emerged. Louis Armstrong—whom you've already met—set the soloist free, while Whiteman, Beiderbecke, Ellington, and others—soon to be introduced to you—developed jazz in ways its founders could never have conceived of. Whatever the need, jazz fulfilled it, producing a plethora of different styles and a galaxy of stars (as well as numerous clichés).

All good things come to an end, and the Jazz Age shuddered to a halt with the Wall Street Crash in 1929 and the onset of the

Depression. The end of Prohibition in 1933 raised spirits, but the froth of those heady dance years was gone.

The wine cellar at the Vanderbilt Hotel in New York during Prohibition: what can he be serving?

The police pooping another potential party. What a terrible waste of good liquor …

The jazz audience

The audience for jazz in the early 1920s was the black working class, but the success of the all-white ODJB brought young, middle-class whites to jazz. King Oliver's sets with Louis Armstrong at the Lincoln Gardens in Chicago became so popular that "midnight rambles" were specially staged on Wednesday nights to cater to white fans. Commercial radio brought another new audience, jukeboxes increased in number, and high-quality jazz records were readily available in the late 1920s. Whoever you were, wherever you went, jazz was what you listened to.

1925 American labor leader A. Philip Randolph organizes the Brotherhood of Sleeping Car Porters to help bring American blacks into the mainstream of the American labor movement.

1926 The glamorous, costumed Broadway revue known as Ziegfeld Follies celebrates its 15th anniversary.

1928 French composer Maurice Ravel composes his popular *Bolero*.

1921~1943

Flying Hands
The Stride Pianists

Fats Waller, the quintessential cheeky guy.

Tootling away somewhere in the background of jazz have been the pianists, usually present but until now rarely heard. As a percussive instrument, the piano has traditionally held a role as part of the rhythm section, keeping time and adding the odd flourish to pep up the tune. Ragtime might have been a piano-led style, but as we've already decided it wasn't really jazz, it doesn't count in the great scheme of things. But now that Armstrong is taking solos, why not pianists? After all, they can play up to ten notes at a time, not just one. So bring on the stride pianists.

S tride piano got its name because, on the four beats of each bar, the left-hand bass line strides between single low notes on the strong beats and answering chords on the weak beats, providing both rhythm and harmony, leaving the right hand free to supply the melody. Sounds complex in print, but once heard never forgotten. Stride grew out of ragtime but had none of its rigidity, giving pianists both the syntax

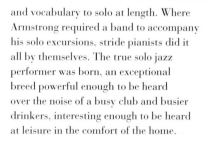

James P. Johnson, a consummate pianist and composer.

In slow motion

Stride piano was a hard style to learn, even for the young Duke Ellington. He only managed to master Johnson's *Carolina Shout* by slowing down his pianola's mechanism so that he could work out the fingering patterns. Fats Waller did the same some years later.

and vocabulary to solo at length. Where Armstrong required a band to accompany his solo excursions, stride pianists did it all by themselves. The true solo jazz performer was born, an exceptional breed powerful enough to be heard over the noise of a busy club and busier drinkers, interesting enough to be heard at leisure in the comfort of the home.

PIANO STARS
Names to conjure with: *James P. Johnson* (1894–1955), the originator and finest exponent of stride, a virtuoso solo performer with tremendous power

1931 Detective Dick Tracy, created by cartoonist Chester Gould, makes his first appearance in the Detroit *Mirror*.

1934 The world's first launderette opens in Texas with four electric washing machines.

1937 Aviator Amelia Earhart, the first woman to fly across the Atlantic Ocean, vanishes on a round-the-world flight.

Star billing for Art Tatum, God's pianist on Earth and a true two-handed wonder.

Art Tatum

Adams's Rules of Jazz advise, among other things, that "genius" should be used sparingly to avoid diluting the word, but in anybody's rule book Art Tatum (1909–56) was a genius. Virtually blind from birth, Tatum had a prodigious, ambidextrous technique that makes him the most orchestral pianist in jazz history. His left hand was an entire rhythm section, both hands together a full-blown big band. By the end of his life, he had long strode past stride, playing two-handed piano that left listeners open-mouthed at his melodic and harmonic invention. No wonder his contemporaries called him God.

and greater invention: in 1923 he wrote *Charleston* for his hit Broadway musical *Runnin' Wild*, thus naming a famous dance. *Willie "The Lion" SMITH* (1897–1973), so called because of his heroism at the front during the Great War, who introduced a classical touch. *Earl "Fatha" HINES* (1903–83), who accompanied Louis Armstrong on his later Hot Five sessions. To some ears, his florid excursions are so much excess froth, but the brew beneath is anything but weak.

Showmen the lot of them, but the greatest offender was *Fats WALLER* (1904–43), equally adept at both piano and organ—he even played jazz on the hallowed pipes of Notre Dame cathedral in Paris. As over-indulgent in life as he was on the keyboard, he kept two bottles of gin on the table during rehearsals, one for himself, the other for his band. Regular top-ups for all kept the music flowing. Ain't Misbehavin'?

ALL THAT JAZZ

JAMES P. JOHNSON—*The Complete Piano Solos, 1921–1939* (Columbia); *Harlem Stride Piano 1921–29* (Hot'N'Sweet).
WILLIE SMITH—*Willie "The Lion" Smith 1938–40* (Classics).
EARL HINES—*Earl Hines Collection: Piano Solos 1928–40* (Collector's Classics).
FATS WALLER—*Piano Solos 1929–41* (RCA, 2 CDs); *The Last Years 1940–43* (RCA Bluebird, 3-CD set).
ART TATUM—*The Art Tatum Solo Masterpieces (1953–55)* (Pablo, 7-CD set).

1923 Harold Lloyd's classic film *Safety Last* is comedy hit of the year.

1924 American industrialist J. D. Rockefeller donates $1 million to New York's Metropolitan Museum of Art.

1925 Frisbee is played for the first time by a group of students using empty Frisbie Baking Company pie plates.

1920~1938
Of Symphonies and Strings
Paul Whiteman

Paul Whiteman looking onward and upward, and standing for no nonsense.

We've got a problem here—or rather, the American music industry has got a problem. With jazz, and with New Orleans jazz in particular, because that sort of jazz is raucous and raunchy and reeks too much of sex. And as we already know, where there's sex, there are problems, always. Looked at from a New York point of view—where the U.S. recording industries were based, and where Tin Pan Alley, the song publishing industry, flourished—New York loved jazz, America loved jazz, but didn't always like the sound it made. In which case, change the sound.

Come the hour, come the man, in this case the aptly named *Paul WHITEMAN* (1890–1967), an educated, musically literate white bandleader from Denver. Scooping up some arrangements by a West Coast pianist called *Ferde GROFÉ* (1892–1972), Whiteman smoothed out the rough edges of jazz with strings and subtle saxophones and plenty of lilting harmonies. Taking jazz by the proverbial scruff, he smartened it up, gave it an elegant suit, and headed it toward the classier dance halls. Huge and immediate success followed. Recorded in 1920, *Whispering*, backed by *Japanese Sandman*, sold a million, as did many more of his songs, and the entertainment industry sighed a big sigh of relief. Classy jazz for the lazy masses at last.

It is of course debatable whether Whiteman's orchestra even played jazz. Most of the musicians had neither the skill nor the inclination to improvise very much, and without the rough edges we're into easy-listening, symphony land here. So much so that Whiteman staged "An Experiment in Modern Music" at New

George Gershwin
Unlike other symphonic jazz composers, Gershwin approached his task from a popular, rather than a classical, background. From 1924 he worked with his brother Ira as librettist to produce a series of brilliant Broadway musicals. *Fascinatin' Rhythm* from 1924's *Lady, Be Good!* and *I Got Rhythm* from 1930's *Girl Crazy* have become jazz standards, while almost every song from his "American folk opera," *Porgy and Bess* (1935), has entered the standard jazz repertoire.

1926 The word "gig," meaning a performance or a booking for a jazz musician, is introduced.

1929 Josephine Baker, dancer and singer, is banned from the Munich stage for indecent behavior.

1930 The jet engine is invented by Sir Frank Whittle.

ALL THAT JAZZ

PAUL WHITEMAN—Paul Whiteman (Jazz Portraits) covers 1920–38, the start and heyday of his career; *When Day Is Done* (Happy Days) includes Gershwin soloing on *Rhapsody in Blue*.

GEORGE GERSHWIN—Recordings of *Rhapsody in Blue* (1924), *An American in Paris* (1928), and *Porgy and Bess* (1935) are too numerous to mention.

JOE VENUTI—*Joe Venuti and Eddie Lang* (Jazz Classics in Digital Stereo; an identically entitled two-volume set on JSP contains more tracks).

H I P C A T S

Hidden within the various Whiteman bands were jazz musicians of distinction. Guitarist **Eddie Lang** *(1902–33) played dapper lines with a lightly rhythmic, sensitive touch. Violinist* **Joe Venuti** *(1903–78) was an unashamed romantic, bringing an infectious, buoyant swing to every phrase he played. Away from the Whiteman band, he and Lang played some excellent small-group jazz. Trombonist* **Jack Teagarden** *(1905–64), later to be a member of Louis Armstrong's All Stars, played as he spoke—long, legato phrases juxtaposed with fluttering arpeggios, relaxed to the point of melancholy but never maudlin. Bix Beiderbecke, Bunny Berigan, and Frankie Trumbauer also passed through the band—of them, more later—as did singer, later crooner,* **Bing Crosby** *(1903–77), given his first break by Whiteman.*

York's Aeolian Concert Hall on February 12, 1924, designed to show how far he had moved from "discordant early jazz to the melodious form of the present." He commissioned *George GERSHWIN* (1898–1937) to write a jazz concerto—*Rhapsody in Blue*—to be performed at the concert, and repeated the experiment seven more times between 1925 and 1938 just to prove his point.

Where Gershwin led, others followed, notably *Aaron COPLAND* (1900–90) and *Leonard BERNSTEIN* (1918–90). Blame it all on Whiteman, but where some saw only pretension, others saw the future of dance music and the wider possibilities of orchestrated jazz that stayed truer to the roots of jazz than Whiteman permitted. Echoes of Whiteman will rebound for many years to come.

The Gershwin boys as portrayed in the Warner Brothers film *Rhapsody in Blue* (1945).

1930 Britain's first public telephone booths come into service in London.

1934 The All England Club in Wimbledon is shocked by women tennis players appearing on the courts in shorts.

1935 Paperback books appear for the first time as Bodley Head publishes its new "Penguin" line.

1923~1959

Enter the Saxophone
Sidney Bechet

Sidney Bechet weaving his magic: a major figure in jazz.

If the transition from cornet to trumpet was almost imperceptible, the contemporary shift from clarinet to saxophone was much more dramatic, and can be traced to a music shop in London's Soho in 1919. There a young New Orleans musician, Sidney BECHET (1897–1959), on tour in Europe with the Southern Syncopated Orchestra, a concert ensemble playing light classics and formal ragtime, spied a soprano saxophone. He bought it, learned to play it, and promptly did for the saxophone what Armstrong did for the trumpet—gave it a language and a style which every successor had to assimilate if not to emulate.

Bechet was easily Armstrong's equal. He was largely self-taught, he could read no music, yet—with no model to go on—invented for the saxophone an approach that swept aside the stiff formalities of ragtime and the simplicities of New Orleans jazz and replaced them with a sinuous, flowing style aided by a biting tone and massive vibrato.

Bechet was an imperious presence with considerable musical skills, and had he stayed in one place for more than a few

ALL THAT JAZZ

Sidney Bechet, 1923–36 and *1937–38* (Classics); the *Complete Sidney Bechet* (RCA, five volumes), covering the years 1932–43; and *Jazz Classics Volumes 1 & 2* (Blue Note), his complete recordings between 1939–51 for the label, including *Summertime*, will give you all you need to hear and more.

years he would now be considered the major jazz player of the interwar years.

But he was an inveterate wanderer, playing in Paris in 1925 as a musician with the Revue Nègre—in which Josephine Baker made such an impression as a dancer—touring Europe (including Russia) for four years, and then, after a lengthy spell in New York, finally returning in 1949 to Paris. He died in Paris ten years later, a French national hero—so much so

1936 In Britain, mass production of gas masks begins.

1947 Howard Hughes's airplane *Spruce Goose*, the largest ever, flies for one mile at an altitude of 80 feet.

1951 Blues singer Muddy Waters has a hit with *Rolling Stone*; the magazine and the famous rock band later derive their names from it.

that a square was named after him in Antibes in the south of France, the location of an annual jazz festival. He was also a bruiser, expelled from both Britain and France for fighting, and he even served a year in a French prison in 1929 for firearms offenses.

Twice, Bechet's career was rescued from oblivion: his recording of George Gershwin's *Summertime* in 1939 after a period working as a tailor reinstated him firmly in the public eye, while his

Clarinet to saxophone

The favored reed instrument of New Orleans jazz musicians was the clarinet: both untutored blacks and better-educated Creoles schooled in the European classical tradition played the instrument as a reedy contrast to the brassy trumpet. During the 1920s the clarinet slowly lost ground to the saxophone, which had been invented by a German, Adolphe Sax, in about 1840. Despite Sax's best intentions, the saxophone was rarely heard in classical compositions, but Gershwin and Copland used it in their symphonic jazz creations. The saxophone's combination of a single-reed mouthpiece and brass body produced a seductively warm sound with an attacking edge ideally suited to jazz, while its shared fingering techniques with the clarinet encouraged many reedsmen, notably Bechet, to transfer their allegiance. Bechet played soprano sax, while others mastered the alto, tenor, or baritone; the bass saxophone is a rare beast. The long dominance of the saxophone in jazz had begun.

appearance at the 1949 Paris Jazz Festival, alongside Charlie Parker and other giants of bebop, showed that he had lost none of his skills. Not until John Coltrane came on the scene in the early 1960s did any other musician approach Bechet's mastery of the soprano saxophone. A main man in every way, in spite of his unwarranted critical and public neglect.

Poster-sized racial stereotypes, but generally Paris was considerably more enlightened than the rest of Europe.

1924 André Breton's Manifesto of Surrealism marks the beginning of the controversial Surrealist movement.

1925 Alban Berg's most famous work, social protest opera *Wozzeck*, premières in Berlin.

1927 Crime novelist Agatha Christie disappears and is found 11 days later having lost her memory. She never accounts for those lost days.

1924~1931

Life's Too Short

Bix Beiderbecke

He abbreviated his name to Bix, and abbreviated his life with alcohol. But since we're talking sex god here, brevity and tragedy are always useful ingredients in the making of a myth. And the myth of Leon Bismarck BEIDERBECKE (1903–31) is one of the bigtime myths of jazz, the beautiful boy from Iowa with the privileged upbringing who rejected a military career and embraced jazz with a vengeance. He recorded fitfully for a mere six years, receiving only two critical notices while alive, and recognized only by fellow musicians and a few fans. Yet he was lionized after death, becoming the first white superstar of jazz.

The golden boy packed a lot into those six years. By the time he was chucked out of his military academy in 1922 he had developed a taste for New Orleans jazz and Prohibition alcohol. He was soon fronting the Wolverines, with whom he made his first recordings in 1924, and sat in with many of the leading jazz musicians of his day, notably Armstrong and Oliver. A couple of big bands later, he joined Paul Whiteman's orchestra, featuring as a soloist from 1928 to 1929, despite increasing absences due to ill health. And then he died, in a boarding house in Queens, New York.

Bix, the beautiful boy, in the early 1920s, while still sober. Pneumonia, aided and abetted by booze, carried him off when he was only 28 years old.

1928 The first color television pictures are transmitted at London's Baird Studios.

1930 Amy Johnson completes her 19-day solo flight from Britain to Australia.

1931 Mickey Mouse receives a special award at the Golden Globe ceremony.

Kirk Douglas stars as Bix in *Young Man with a Horn* (1950), Hollywood's contribution to the Beiderbecke mythology industry.

His recordings reveal a burnished, bell-like sound that his friend Hoagy Carmichael described as a chime being struck by a mallet. His delivery was cool and understated, his flowing lines possessed of pure logic, yet such was his natural ability that he never learned to read music properly. He composed only five pieces, all for piano, but during his lifetime his reputation among the jazz fraternity was such that he became the first white musician ever to be admired—and imitated—by black musicians, trumpeter Rex

Man to myth

The process of turning Beiderbecke the man into Beiderbecke the enduring myth began with the publication in 1938 of Dorothy Baker's novel *Young Man with a Horn*, which was very loosely based on his life and career. Since then, a flood of memoirs, biographies, critical appreciations, and even a 1950 film starring Kirk Douglas have added to the pile of memorabilia.

H I P   C A T S

Bix's partner in crime was saxophonist **Frankie Trumbauer** *(1901–56)—Tram for short. The two first worked together in the orchestra of* **Jean Goldkette** *(1899–1962) and continued their association with Paul Whiteman. Like two peas in a pod, Bix and Tram both produced superbly phrased solos to order, Tram possessing a light tone and virtuoso technical ability. Tram was also a skilled pilot, flying his own plane to gigs. Unlike his solos, he didn't always manage to stay airborne, crashing into the hotel in St. Louis in which he was meant to be playing after the plane developed engine trouble. The career of trumpeter* **Bunny Berigan** *(1908–42) was almost a mirror image to that of Bix; both were white, both highly skilled, yet both drank themselves to death at an early age. Unlike Bix, Berigan has remained a little-known jazz figure, despite playing masterful trumpet with a sweet-and-sour tone and great rhythmic drive.*

Stewart and others learning to play his famous solo from *Singin' the Blues* note for note. Through his solos he defined a style best described as cool, a label which did not properly establish itself until the 1950s, twenty years after his death. Listen to a solo by Bix Beiderbecke, and what you hear is the sound of the Jazz Age he personified. Pure genius.

1924 The system of "seeding" tennis players is used at Wimbledon for the first time.

1925 The *Exposition des Arts Décoratifs* takes place in Paris, displaying Art Deco designs and fashions.

1929 Kellogg's, fast becoming a worldwide success, launches its "snap, crackle, and pop" breakfast cereal, Rice Krispies.

1923~1933
Singin' the Blues
Bessie Smith and Ma Rainey

So far, it's all been jazz. And so far, mainly men. So it's about time that we introduce the blues, and with it two magnificent women singers. But what has blues got to do with jazz, and where has it been all this time?

The Blues

Sorry to be difficult here, but if you're after a single definition of the blues, there isn't one. The blues are a state of mind, and the music expressing that state of mind, and numerous musical structures used to perform that music, and the performance itself. Think, play, sing, or act the blues—it's all the blues. But to simplify matters a bit, when jazz musicians talk of the blues, they are usually referring to a basic 12-bar form divided into three four-bar sections, involving a harmonic progression through chords on the first, fourth, and fifth notes of the scale. A simple blues song using this progression has a single line sung over four bars, then repeated over four more bars, with a final four-bar rhyming response. Numerous variations of this formula exist. The distinctive blues sound is achieved by lowering the third, seventh, and sometimes fifth, notes of the scale, thus creating "blue notes," a defining sound of both blues and jazz music. All very off-putting on paper, but once heard, you'll soon identify blue notes and blues songs across any crowded bar.

The simple answer is that, like jazz, blues was not recorded until late (in its case, 1920), so we don't know much about its early history. It was probably derived from songs sung on the plantations—initially sung unaccompanied, then played with a single instrument such as a guitar or banjo trading melodic phrases with the vocalist. By the turn of the century, the form had developed into

Now listen here ... Nat King Cole as W.C. Handy gets it in the neck in *St. Louis Blues* (1958).

a three-line verse sung over a 12-bar pattern. Jazz musicians used the blues format as a vehicle for improvisation, so that by the 1920s the blues was a recognized sub-genre of jazz.

Compared with jazz, blues was primitive in form, but in the hands of its early practitioners it could be magnificent music.

1930 Marlene Dietrich shoots to stardom with the release of *The Blue Angel*, a film in which she plays seductive cabaret singer Lola.

1931 *The Star Spangled Banner* is adopted as the American national anthem.

1933 The mass exodus from Germany includes composers Arnold Schoenberg and Kurt Weill, conductor Otto Klemperer, writers Bertolt Brecht and Thomas Mann, director Fritz Lang, and artists Paul Klee and Wassily Kandinsky.

Nobody messed with Bessie Smith, the magnificent "Empress of the Blues."

Where Bessie Smith was chic, *Ma Rainey* (1886–1939) was, well, earthy. She toured regularly throughout the southern states on the TOBA circuit (the Theater Owners Booking Association, also known as Tough On Black Artists)—the only source of entertainment in many black towns—and recorded close to a hundred songs. With a majestic delivery, a simple but dramatic voice, often melancholic in tone, and an uncanny ability to read and respond to her audience, she was, for many people, the blues personified.

In February 1923 *Bessie Smith* (1895–1937) recorded *Down-Hearted Blues*, which quickly sold over three-quarters of a million copies and earned her a nine-year recording contract with Columbia. The "Empress of the Blues" was awe-inspiring, with great dramatic presence, a voice covering the full gamut of emotions, and the ability to get inside every song and make it her own. She earned $2,000 a week at the height of her career and worked with all the jazz greats.

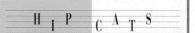

H I P C A T S

W. C. Handy *(1873–1958) regarded himself as the "Father of the Blues," composing, or at least copyrighting, numerous blues pieces, notably* Memphis Blues *(1912) and* St. Louis Blues *(1914), which have since become jazz standards. In 1920* **Mamie Smith** *(1883–1946) recorded the first blues record by a black singer—*Crazy Blues*—which was a huge success, paving the way for Bessie Smith and Ma Rainey. Compared to these superstars,* **Robert Johnson** *(1911–38) was an unknown. He recorded a mere 29 songs before he was murdered (by a man whose wife Johnson was having an affair with), but those songs—notably* Love in Vain *and* Cross Roads Blues*—have exerted a powerful, some say demonic, influence on all subsequent blues singers and on numerous rock groups.*

1925 Anita Loos's novel *Gentlemen Prefer Blondes* is published. It is later made into a musical starring Marilyn Monroe and Jane Russell.

1926 The Harlem Globetrotters basketball team is organized by Abe Saperstein in Chicago.

1931 The Empire State Building, the world's tallest building, opens in New York City.

1920~1940
The Big Apple
New York City

Park Avenue, New York, 1935: tall, open, and fast for jazz.

Bright lights, big city, skyscrapers, melting pots—we're in New York at last, a city about to stamp its indelible mark on jazz all the way up to the present day. For as the black migration north filled up the city in the early years of this century, jazz flowed in as well. New York being New York, however, its jazz was different. The city was home to the American entertainment industry—Broadway, Tin Pan Alley, the record industry—so jazz had to compete in the deliverance of pleasure. But variety is strength, and with so much life on the ground, jazz had plenty to nourish it.

Rent parties

Landlord coming at the end of the week? No money to pay the rent? No problem. Lay on some food and drink, get in a stride pianist or blues musician to play some good-time tunes, and charge your friends for the privilege of crossing the threshold. End of the week, you've got a mighty hangover, your neighbors are still complaining about the noise, but the landlord's got his rent and the apartment's yours, at least for another week. Ain't nothin' goin' on but the rent, indeed.

Two main sources of food—Harlem and the dance hall—gave jazz its healthy glow. Harlem, in north Manhattan, was the largest black community in the U.S., and during the 1920s it enjoyed a cultural explosion later termed the Harlem Renaissance. Black musicians, writers, poets (notably Langston Hughes), artists, and performers found a ready audience in the district, fueled

Court jester: dental perfection from Cab Calloway, one of the Cotton Club's resident stars.

1933 President Roosevelt orders all banks in the United States to be temporarily closed after the Wall Street Crash.

1934 Charles Darrow's board game "Monopoly" passes go and becomes an instant success. The original design used street names from Atlantic City, New Jersey.

1938 Irving Berlin's song *God Bless America* is heard for the first time, sung by Kate Smith on her radio show.

by a potent brew of illegal drink and black consciousness politics. Here were the Cotton Club and other clubs and dives, attracting vast numbers of locals, plus white Manhattanites, in their eyes slumming uptown for the night. Those locals too poor to go clubbing made their own entertainment at improvised rent parties and parlor socials.

Across the city, dance halls flourished, but the music the dancers demanded was neither the raucous romp of New Orleans nor its smooth (some might say bland) antithesis developed by Paul Whiteman. Race records aimed at the black market were creating a huge audience for blues singers, and jazz musicians soon learned from them a more emotional delivery. Picking up on this trend, bandleader *Fletcher* HENDERSON (1897–1952), a chemistry graduate from Georgia who had begun as a

The Cotton Club

The most famous jazz club in the world opened in Harlem in 1920 as the Club Deluxe. Owned at first by Jack Johnson, the first black heavyweight champion of the world, it was taken over in 1922 by Owney Madden, who changed its name to the Cotton Club. It remained at the same venue—644 Lenox Avenue—until 1936, when it closed pending relocation south to West 48th Street in Manhattan, after race riots in Harlem the previous year had scared away most of its white clientele. The club survived in its new venue until it closed for good in 1940.

In those two decades, the Cotton Club personified New York nightlife. The cream of society came to its glittering theatrical revues, which provided employment for numerous jazz musicians. Star attractions were the resident house bands: Andy Preer's Cotton Club Syncopators until 1927, then Ellington, followed by Cab Calloway and his Missourians from 1931, and finally, Jimmie Lunceford's band after 1934.

Whiteman clone, brought Louis Armstrong to New York in 1924 to spice up his band with some jazz. The city was electrified by Armstrong's appearance, and where Henderson led, others followed. Most notably, Duke Ellington (see p. 38), whose four-year residency at the Cotton Club from 1927 playing big band "jungle music" soon become the stuff of legend.

Shake a leg and count to six: the Jivin' Lindy Hoppers at the Cotton Club.

1928 German playwright Bertolt Brecht's controversial play *The Threepenny Opera*, with musical score by Kurt Weill, opens in Berlin and is enthusiastically received.

1933 The first photographs of the Loch Ness monster are published in Britain's *Daily Mail*.

1934 Engineer Percy Shaw introduces the reflective "catseye" safety feature to British roads.

1923~1974

The Duke

Edward Kennedy Ellington

To do justice to Edward Kennedy "Duke" ELLINGTON (1899–1974) would require several books, such is his all-around importance. He might have been born the son of a butler in Washington, D.C., in 1899, had little formal musical training, and learned his skills in the clubs of Harlem. But from such a start came Ellington the sophisticate and snappy dresser, the composer and arranger, the first-class pianist, the band leader and organizer, the entertainer and artist, the alchemist of sound, and all-around genius of jazz until his death in 1974.

Duke Ellington: urbane, sophisticated, and ducally hip.

HIP CATS

*Passing through the Ellington band on its long career were some of the finest jazz musicians of their day. Trumpeter **James "Bubber" Miley** and trombonist **Joe "Tricky Sam" Nanton** gave the band its initial vocalized jungle growl during the 1920s, while alto saxophonist **Johnny Hodges** and baritone saxophonist **Harry Carney** added a romantic sheen in the 1930s. The arrival in the band in 1939–40 of bassist **Jimmy Blanton** and tenor saxophonist **Ben Webster** added further range, completed by the compositions and arrangements of **Billy Strayhorn**. Tenor sax player **Paul Gonsalves** revitalized the band in the 1950s.*

Ellington's compositions total more than 2,000. Large-scale suites?—well over 20 to choose from. Religious works?—three sacred concerts. Film and TV scores?—six at least. Musicals and stage works?—seven and more. Operas?—one, *Boola*, unfinished and unperformed. Short instrumental pieces?—well over 1,000. Popular songs?—hundreds. Prolific is the word, for he composed not at the piano but on the road, scribbling madly whenever he got the chance. And famous, too, for his songs are the classics of jazz. Pseudo-African jungle ditties like *East St. Louis Toodle-oo* (1927) and *The Mooche* (1928), ballads like *Mood Indigo* (1930) and *In a Sentimental Mood* (1935), up-tempo swingers like *Rockin' in Rhythm* (1930)

1935 Kreuger launches the first canned beer in New York.

1950 Composer, musician, and singer James Cleveland becomes the first black gospel artist to appear at Carnegie Hall.

1972 Federal Express is founded by Frederick W. Smith, a Memphis businessman.

The suites

Ellington wrote suites for a jazz orchestra the way other people write shopping lists. He started tentatively, with two versions of the short *Creole Rhapsody*, both of which extended the original song over two sides of a 78-rpm disk. In 1943 he premièred *Black, Brown and Beige*, a five-section tone-poem portraying the history of black people in the U.S. By the mid-1940s the format was well established—four or more sections of related variations on a theme that painted a composite musical portrait. When the concerts ended in 1952, he exploited the new LP format to enshrine his suites on vinyl.

and *It Don't Mean a Thing If It Ain't Got That Swing* (1932)—they just kept on coming. And when he paused for breath, Billy Strayhorn took over, composing the atmospheric *Take the A Train* (1941), which became the band's theme song.

But Ellington was not just a great songwriter. He was also a composer and arranger of sound, using a wide palette of instrumental effects to craft extraordinary performances from his musicians. While at the Cotton Club, 1927–31, he led the band through dance-theater jungle routines, developing a more sentimental repertoire as the 1930s wore on. His greatest period was in the early 1940s, when Blanton, Webster, Hodges, *et al.* were on stage. Like many big bands—this one comprising 18 players by 1946—the Ellington orchestra fell out of favor after the war, but staged a magnificent comeback at the 1956 Newport Jazz Festival, when tenor saxophonist Paul Gonsalves ran through

27 jaw-dropping choruses of *Diminuendo and Crescendo in Blue* as if the band had never gone away. After that, Ellington became a jazz institution, publicly admired and occasionally sniped at. A man for all seasons, and in every season something to suit everybody.

The bass

During the late 1920s, bassists such as Walter Page (1900–57) of Count Basie's band developed the "walking bass," playing all four beats of the bar in stepwise fashion. But a revolution in bass-playing occurred in 1939 when Jimmy Blanton (1918–42) joined Duke Ellington's orchestra. He played runs of notes behind the soloists, complementing the piano by enlarging the accompaniment, and taking solos himself. His early death robbed jazz of one its finest improvisers.

ALL THAT JAZZ

So much to listen to, so little space to describe it. Bear in mind that a song recorded in the 1930s will not sound the same played 30 years later with a different band. That said, the following will do to be getting on with: *Early Ellington 1927–1934* (RCA Bluebird); *Jungle Nights in Harlem* (RCA Bluebird); *The Blanton–Webster Band* (RCA Bluebird, 3 CDs), covering 1940–42; *Black, Brown and Beige* (RCA Bluebird, 3 CDs); *Ellington at Newport* (Columbia): the famous concert; *And His Mother Called Him Bill* (Bluebird), a poignant 1967 tribute to Billy Strayhorn.

Ben Webster: the laid-back man with the saxophone.

1930 Frozen peas, the first successful frozen vegetable, go on sale.

1931 German film *Mädchen in Uniform* (Girls in Uniform) is the first film to portray lesbian love.

1932 Radio City Music Hall opens in New York.

1930~1935

Ready to Swing
The Big Band Era

Blaring trumpets and gruff trombones answered by roaring saxophones, a powerhouse rhythm section driving all before it, groups of musicians in uniforms bobbing up and down on the bandstand as their section took its turn to play, a star soloist stepping forward to take the applause—this is the big band in action, and the early 1930s saw the start of its dominance in jazz.

> **Swing**
> Swing is a slippery concept to define. Think of it as the tension created between the basic beat of the music and the actual notes and emphases played by the musicians. That tension creates the forward propulsion known as swing. Call it a natural jazz rhythm or a relaxed state of mind, swing just grabs you when you hear it. Trust me.

Ironic, really, that big bands should flourish in the 1930s, for the Depression was knocking America's economy flat. Bechet took up shoe-shining and managed a tailor's shop, Armstrong and Ellington went to Europe to look for work, and those big bands that survived worked for peanuts or, like the Austin High School Gang, ate baked beans. But in the midst of poverty, dancing was always a cheap entertainment, and after the abolition of Prohibition in 1933, it was at least legal to drink again.

What dancers needed was music that swung, and big bands had plenty of swing

Art Deco designer jazz, 1930s style: Jimmie Lunceford's Band.

1933 Prohibition ends on February 5, and 1.5 million barrels of beer are drunk in the U.S. that night.

1934 Englishman Richard Hardy complains that the English language is becoming tainted by trends for words such as "definitely," "frightfully," "absolutely," "awfully," and "priceless."

1935 RADAR (Radio Detection and Ranging) is demonstrated in secret in Britain.

H I P   C A T S

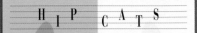

Some names of early big bands to conjure with: **Fletcher Henderson** *(1897–1952) and his arranger* **Don Redman** *(1900–64) led the big-band field, but the bands of* **Chick Webb** *(1909–39),* **Earl Hines** *(1903–83),* **Jimmie Lunceford** *(1902–47), and Panamanian-born* **Luis Russell** *(1902–63) weren't too far behind. These and many other big bands acted like schools for promising musicians, setting them up to make it on their own later.*

By 1935 the big-band swing formula was perfected, but some of its practitioners lacked mass appeal. Come the hour, come the King of Swing. In the hands of Mr. Benny Goodman, swing was set to conquer the world.

to spare. They achieved it by taking the tension of a Louis Armstrong small group—solos against the underlying rhythm of the band—and translating it into a big-band format. As the rhythm section laid down the beat, the brass and reeds sang out the melody, quietly at first, then louder. Tension was increased by setting the sections against each other, brass and reeds exchanging riffs, or little phrases, calling and responding at ever-increasing volumes. Finally a soloist would blow, roaring around the melody and over the massed musicians before subsiding back into the band amid tumultuous applause. The energy created was electric, and with an audience on its feet the bands were revved up and ready to swing all night.

Chick Webb, leading the big-band beat from behind.

The big bands
A typical 1930s band would have 14 or 15 members—trumpets, trombones, saxophones, and a four-piece rhythm section of piano, guitar, double bass, and drums, as well as the bandleader. After 1935 the economic upturn spurred bandleaders to increase the size of their bands, and some leaders introduced orchestral instruments such as French horns, flutes, and violins for added texture. Out of this huge ensemble, bands within bands were created, stepping forward to play a short set of more intimate pieces, giving everyone a breather. The Benny Goodman small groups are the best known of these little big bands.

1935 The Marx Brothers hilarious film *Night at the Opera* is released.

1936 British monarch King Edward VIII abdicates in order to marry American divorcee Wallis Simpson.

1937 The first British television broadcasts are made from Alexandra Palace in north London.

1935~1940

The King of Swing
Benny Goodman

The story goes like this. In August 1935 the Benny Goodman band, packed to the gills with star musicians, was on tour in southern California, where its reception was less than enthusiastic. The band opened its show at the Palomar Ballroom in Los Angeles by playing soft dance music. The largely white audience of college students was unimpressed, so Goodman led the band into an up-tempo, full-throttle arrangement of Jelly Roll Morton's King Porter Stomp. *The audience went wild, as did the vast numbers listening to the music on the radio, and swing soon swept the nation. The King of Swing was born.*

HIP CATS

Goodman's band included such fine musicians as pianist **Teddy Wilson** *(1912–86), the exuberant vibraphonist* **Lionel Hampton** *(b.1909), and drummer* **Gene Krupa** *(1909–73), who together played with Goodman as a quartet within the band. White bandleaders who benefited from Goodman's success included fellow clarinetist* **Artie Shaw** *(b.1910), famous for his performance of* Begin the Beguine *(1938); the* **Dorsey** *brothers* **Jimmy** *(1904–57) and* **Tommy** *(1905–56);* **Bob Crosby** *(1913–93);* **Harry James** *(1916–83); and* **Glenn Miller** *(1904–44). Several of these bands featured singers, most notably* **Frank Sinatra** *(1915–98), who sang with both* **Harry James's** *and* **Tommy Dorsey's** *bands, and* **Peggy Lee**, *who sang with Goodman. Confusingly,* **Bing Crosby** *(1903–77) sang with Paul Whiteman, not with his brother Bob.*

Benny GOODMAN (1909–86) was an unlikely jazz star—a white, Jewish, brash, domineering clarinet player. But he was also younger than the average jazz musician and appealed to an increasingly educated audience that appreciated his band's mixture of tight, driving swing and flawless musicianship.

Benny Goodman with drummer Gene Krupa and pianist Teddy Wilson.

1938 Supermarket shopping carts are introduced for the first time, in Oklahoma.

1939 Marian Anderson, well-known contralto, is refused permission to perform at the Constitution Hall, Washington, D.C., because she is black.

1940 English phrasebooks are issued to German troops in preparation for the invasion of Britain.

Jiving it up at the Savoy Ballroom, Harlem.

Jazz guitar

As Jimmy Blanton was to the double bass, so Charlie Christian (1916–42) was to the guitar. Until Christian, the guitar was solely a rhythm instrument, replacing the banjo in the early 1930s. Its lack of volume restricted its use, but Christian was among the first to specialize in amplified guitar. A member of the Goodman band after 1939, he shone in its spin-off sextet, where he played runs of notes with effortless swing and melodic invention. He influenced all the important guitarists for the next 30 years.

delivered by a leader whose love of the classics showed through in his precise intonation. Goodman was the first jazz musician to pursue a parallel career in classical music, and he commissioned works from such composers as Bartók, Copland, and Hindemith, as well as performed and recorded clarinet pieces by Mozart, Stravinsky, and other classical composers. He might have been a control freak and a perfectionist, and many musicians left his band after savage arguments, but he was also brave enough to hire black musicians at a time when mixed-race groups were frowned upon.

Goodman's triumph was in the unlikely setting of New York's Carnegie Hall, where in January 1938 he organized the first-ever jazz concert in a prestigious classical-music venue. The program illustrated the history

of jazz, and included a parody of the Original Dixieland Jazz Band's early recordings. Asked how long an intermission he required, Goodman replied, "How long does Mr. Toscanini take?" The word for Mr. Goodman is chutzpah.

ALL THAT JAZZ

TOMMY DORSEY—*Tommy Dorsey & His Orchestra with Frank Sinatra* (RCA Tribune, 2 CDs)
BENNY GOODMAN—*The Birth of Swing 1935–36* (RCA Bluebird, 3 CDs); *After You've Gone* (RCA Bluebird): the Goodman quartet, 1935–37; *Live at Carnegie Hall* (Columbia, 2 CDs): the famous 1938 concert
GLENN MILLER—*The Popular Recordings 1938–42* (RCA Bluebird)
ARTIE SHAW—*Begin the Beguine* (RCA Bluebird)

1936 Black American athlete Jesse Owens wins four gold medals at the Olympic Games in Berlin. Hitler leaves the stadium and refuses to be photographed with him.

1938 Airmen experience problems with leaky fountain pens at high altitude; George Biro comes up with a solution—the first ballpoint pen.

1943 The frenetic new dance, the jitterbug, takes American dance floors by storm.

1936~1950
One O'Clock Jump
Count Basie

Count Basie, a leading member of the jazz aristocracy, making a polished impression at the piano.

Less equals more tells you everything you need to know about the kid from Red Bank, New Jersey. While other pianists, then as now, sprayed notes all around the keyboard, William "Count" BASIE (1904–84) was minimalism itself; the odd chord, a few well-chosen notes, or a short melodic phrase from the right hand, a quiet stab from the left hand, was all he required to stamp his mark on his surroundings. Sparse to the point of meanness, his playing was light, airy, and swung like the proverbial.

Basie's band, 16 strong by 1937, was similarly sparse in performance, with plenty of space for soloists and a notable reliance on riffs—repeated short melodic phrases—exchanged between the sections. And although many of its brass and reed players were well known, it was most famous for its rhythm section, so highly regarded it came to be known as the All-American Rhythm Section. Alongside Basie on piano, *Walter PAGE* (1900–57) played walking bass lines that buoyed up the whole band. *Jo JONES* (1911–85) revolutionized the role of the drums, and *Freddie GREEN* (1911–87) provided an understated, rhythmically precise accompaniment on guitar that complemented the driving pulse of Jones and Page. The section played four even beats to the bar,

Jazz drumming
The main role of a drummer in early jazz music was to mark time on the bass drum. Cymbal and snare drum provided punctuation and ornament. Basie's drummer Jo Jones changed all this by using the hi-hat, a pair of horizontally mounted cymbals. He transferred the basic pulse to the hi-hat, leaving it slightly open to produce a light, continuous sound, unlike the staccato bass drum beat of earlier drummers. Playing four evenly stressed notes in each bar, Jones used the other drums for punctuation. He also used brushes rather than sticks, giving his playing a light, airy feel that suited the Basie band to perfection.

1947 In the U.S. the first aerosol food product, Reddi-Whip, is introduced.

1948 The Nationalist government in South Africa introduces apartheid, a rigid system of racial segregation.

1948 Leading Soviet composers Sergei Prokofiev and Dmitry Shostakovich are criticized for "ideological laxity."

HIP CATS

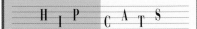

It wasn't just the rhythm section that attracted attention in Basie's band. Trumpeter **Buck Clayton** *(b.1911) possessed a burnished tone and a sensitive style, making him ideal to accompany singers. Trombonist* **Benny Morton** *(1907–85) provided weight to the brass section, while vocalist* **Jimmy Rushing** *(1902–72) sang the blues with a strong jazz intonation. Saxophonists* **Herschel Evans** *(1909–39) and* **Lester Young** *(1909–59), of whom much more later, were polar opposites in both style and personality; Evans's rich, impassioned, forceful delivery in sharp contrast to the light touch of Young. The tension between the two made the band crackle.*

broke up on tour in 1927 in Kansas City. Stranded away from home, Basie joined a local group led by Walter Page and then a big band led by *Bennie MOTEN* (1894–1935). After Moten's death, Basie took the band over, renamed it, and brought it back to the East Coast and fame.

Herschel Evans, the energetic partner (alongside light-fingered Lester Young) in the saxophone pair that fronted the Basie band.

delivered with a lightness of touch that gave the band enormous bounce and a propulsive swing. To perfect its technique, the section practiced by itself for hours. Once wound up, it ran like clockwork.

KANSAS CITY

Confusingly for someone who came from New Jersey, Count Basie's band defined the Kansas City sound—simpler, lighter, and bluesier, although no less intense, than the highly organized, musically advanced Goodman or Ellington bands in New York. Basie's own connection with Kansas was pure accident—a band he was a member of

ALL THAT JAZZ

The Original American Decca Recordings (MCA, 3 CDs) catch the band at the height of its powers, 1937–39. *Count Basie 1932–40* (Jazz Classics in Digital Stereo, two volumes) and *The Essential Count Basie* (Columbia, three volumes), spanning the years 1936–41, cover much the same ground.

1922 James Joyce's novel *Ulysses* is banned in Britain and the US because of its use of bad language and explicit descriptions of urination, defecation, and genitalia.

1923 Congress approves a law making all Native Americans citizens of the United States.

1934 In Britain a decision is made to give all schoolchildren half a pint of milk a day as part of a national policy to improve nutrition.

1922~1969
Body and Soul
Coleman Hawkins

What Louis Armstrong was to the trumpet and Sidney Bechet to the soprano saxophone, Coleman HAWKINS (1901–69) was to the tenor saxophone. Before him, almost nothing, for the tenor saxophone was a rare creature in the early jazz world, its clumsy, ungainly sound out of place alongside the lithe clarinets and upfront trumpets. After him, the tenor was the defining sound of jazz, its emotional tone and majestic presence what most people think jazz is all about.

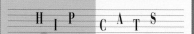

*Hawkins was a loner, never collecting a coterie of musicians around him, and never staying in one place for too long. His all-encompassing style can be heard in the work of **Ben Webster** (1909–73), one of the mainstays of the Ellington band after 1940 and a great romantic player with a sensual, breathy tone. During the 1930s and again in the 1960s, Hawkins collaborated with **Benny Carter** (b.1907), a multi-instrumentalist and arranger who, like Hawkins, updated his style in keeping with the bop revolution.*

Adolphe Sax's invention has been a uniquely expressive tool in jazz.

Coleman Hawkins served as the bridge over which every succeeding tenor saxophonist has crossed. He gave the instrument its vocabulary and grammar, indeed its very sound, playing with a warm, rich tone that owed more to Armstrong's trumpet than to any saxophonist.

Atmosphere for Lovers and Thieves: Ben Webster serves up the usual mix of sex and crime.

He improvised on chords rather than just the melody, playing double-tempo runs of notes and quick-fire triplets and arpeggios—the notes of the chord played one after another in quick succession—that together with blinding melodic improvisation fashioned a solo which soared above the band in tumultuous fashion. Not for nothing was his nickname the Hawk. But he also fashioned a romantic ballad style—most notably in *Body and Soul* (1939), which remains, for many people, the most perfect jazz performance ever recorded, its two-chorus solo a masterpiece of poise and precision.

1947 Raytheon Co. introduces the first commercial microwave oven.

1956 Rock 'n' roll star Elvis Presley takes his first film role in the Western *Love Me Tender*, in which he gets shot and later returns as a singing ghost.

1969 Teddy Kennedy dashes his hopes of presidential election when he drives his car off a bridge on Chappaquiddick Island, Massachusetts, drowning his companion, Mary Jo Kopechne.

To have done all this before reaching middle age would, for most people, be reason enough to settle down, but Hawkins was one of those rare players whose style keeps evolving as they grow older. Though rooted in the music of the swing era, he was in at the birth of bop music in the early 1940s and recorded with all the stars of that adventurous style—his was the first bop recording ever, in 1944. In 1947 he recorded an unaccompanied improvisation—*Picasso*—that was technically demanding even by the high standards of bop, and truly avant-garde in its conception. Meetings with old tenor stars such as Ben Webster and new ones such as Sonny Rollins kept him ahead of the pack, while a bossa nova album recorded in 1962 proved his commercial antennae were still in good order.

In many ways, Hawkins was the jazz man for all seasons, his huge foghorn tone and commanding presence evoking images of jazz itself. With a few notable exceptions, you will have heard every tenor sax solo here first.

Coleman Hawkins plays alongside a young Miles Davis in 1945.

Body and soul

No one's counted, but *Body and Soul* must be one of the most recorded of all American popular songs—more than 3,000 different versions by the time it celebrated its 50th birthday in 1980, another thousand or so since then, no doubt. The song became famous as a showstopper in a 1930 Broadway review called *Three's a Crowd*, but it was nearly cut from the show at warm-up performances in Philadelphia. Lyricists Robert Sour and Edward Heyman tried out several sets of lyrics before Libby Holman sang it into history in New York. Johnny Green's music is complex, with three key changes in both verse and chorus and much winding between major and minor keys, but it is a perfect vehicle for a jazz soloist, even if Coleman Hawkins's famous version suspended the melody almost entirely.

ALL THAT JAZZ

COLEMAN HAWKINS—*Body and Soul* (RCA Bluebird), a selection of recordings 1939–56, including the title song; *Coleman Hawkins: Verve Jazz Masters 34* (Verve), which includes *Picasso*; *Coleman Hawkins Encounters Ben Webster* (Verve): two masters head to head in 1959; *Desafinado* (MCA), on which Hawk plays bossa nova, with style.

SONNY ROLLINS—*All the Things You Are* (RCA Bluebird): the Hawk meets the new wave in 1963.

BEN WEBSTER—*Music for Loving* (Verve, 2 CDs) and *The Soul of Ben Webster* (Verve, 2 CDs) collect the best of Webster from the 1950s; *Atmosphere for Lovers and Thieves* (Black Lion, LP only).

1937 Spam, canned processed pork and ham, is launched by the Hormel Company.

1942 Glenn Miller receives the first gold record for selling one million copies of *Chattanooga Choo Choo.*

1947 The Central Intelligence Agency (CIA) is created by President Truman.

1936~1959

The Pres
Lester Young

A porkpie hat on his head, a tenor sax held at a rakish angle to his right, a strange way of talking and a totally individual way of playing, Lester YOUNG (1909–59) was the bohemian high priest of hip. He was also the man unfortunate enough to play tenor sax at a time when Coleman Hawkins was on top. When Young took over from Hawkins in the Fletcher Henderson band in 1934, he suffered the indignity of being criticized for not sounding like his predecessor. Fletcher's wife even played him old Hawkins records to inspire him to toughen up his sound.

Shall we try it this way? Lester Young could make it work any old way, and always preferred to take his own idiosyncratic angle on things.

L ester Young's playing was everything Hawkins's was not, a cool, avuncular contrast to the macho bluster of the Hawk. His tone was light, laid-back, and even diffident. With off-center timing, he approached a solo sideways, ignoring the bar lines to fill an entire bar with a single note, a few bars with a long phrase, and

Eyes and bells

Idiosyncratic in everything he did, Young had his own hip language for fellow musicians, or "ladies," as he called them all. Billie Holiday was "Lady Day," Buddy Tate was "Moon," Count Basie "The Holy Main." Later, he coped with the pressures of life with a monosyllabic language in which "eyes" indicated desire and "bells" approval. By the end of his life, he had totally withdrawn. In 1958 he planned an album with arranger Gil Evans. "He wanted to make the album," remembered Evans, "but he wanted to die more."

1948 Norwegian anthropologist Thor Heyerdahl completes a 101-day journey across more than 4,000 miles of the Pacific on the *Kon-Tiki*, a balsa raft.

1949 The world's first disposable diapers, Paddipads, are introduced by Robinson's, in Britain.

1956 American movie star Gary Cooper meets artist Pablo Picasso out walking and asks for his autograph.

then silence for a few bars. One critic has remarked that it was like telling stories by parable—through innuendo and euphemism, you quickly got the meaning. Remarkably, he developed this laid-back style while playing against the freewheeling romp of the Basie big band, whose lead soloist he was from 1936, but he never had to shout to make himself heard. Alongside his work with the big band, he partnered Billie Holiday, an ideal match in that both of them had an oblique way of phrasing and the same relaxed, behind-the-beat approach to a line.

HIP CATS

You can hear the immediate legacy of Young in the youthful playing of four saxophonists who came to prominence in the 1940s. **Dexter Gordon** *(1923–89), who once remarked that he gave up playing the tenor for two years after first hearing Young, took Young's style into the bop era, in particular into the band led by Billy Eckstein in 1944. There he had head-to-head blowing contests with* **Gene Ammons** *(1925–74), another Young disciple. Gordon went on to partner* **Wardell Gray** *(1921–55), who started with the tone and style of Young but later fell under Charlie Parker's spell. Closest of all the disciples was* **Paul Quinichette** *(1916–83), whose sound was so similar that he became known as the "Vice-Pres."*

THE ALTERNATIVE LESTER

The Alternative Lester: but in truth there are no alternatives to the brilliantly sideways style of "The President."

DECLINE OF A PRESIDENT

Life went downhill for Pres ("The President," Billie Holiday's nickname for him) when he was drafted into the army in 1944, busted for smoking marijuana, court-martialed, and placed in detention. Although not immediately apparent, the sudden shift from bohemian to regimented lifestyle proved catastrophic to him. His decline was gradual, but slowly more pronounced, as his once-dancing tone grew heavier and more expressive. Yet he lived to see a generation of musicians who owed everything to him. Even after his death, his influence lived on: soul singer Marvin Gaye credits him on the liner notes to *What's Going On* as the man who taught him to sing quietly and just relax. For, as everyone said, he was such a nice man, "a beautiful, beautiful person." That can't be said about every jazz musician.

1934 George Gershwin's musical *Porgy and Bess* opens in New York City.

1939 Hattie McDaniel wins an Oscar for her portrayal of the character Mammy, Scarlett O'Hara's maid, in *Gone with the Wind*.

1940 The exiled Russian war minister Leon Trotsky is axed to death in Mexico by Spaniard Ramon Mercador del Rio.

1933~1959
Lady Day
Billie Holiday

The public, smiling face of Billie Holiday, masking hard times.

For many people, Billie HOLIDAY (1915–59) is the jazz lifestyle personified. Drink, drugs, prostitution, racism, unhappy relationships, abuse—all featured throughout her short life. The trademark gardenia in her hair hid a burn from a hair-curling iron inflicted when she fell asleep before a performance; the long white gloves covered needle trackmarks on her arms. And so on, endlessly and pitifully. But this amazing woman deserves respect for the one thing that made her so distinctive—her voice.

It was a voice like no other in jazz, and for those who have never heard it before, it comes as a great shock. It was a small, worldly voice with a limited range and a strange timbre, exuding a blend of vulnerability and sexuality. Yet that voice "rang like a bell and went a mile," utterly distinct and completely individual. Holiday was entirely self-taught, and admitted only to admiring Bessie Smith's feeling and Louis Armstrong's style. In a way she wasn't a singer at all, for hers was a musicianship of rhythm and melody, not voice. But she

ALL THAT JAZZ

Checkbooks are necessary at this point, as so many of Holiday's songs have been collected into vast, comprehensive, and expensive boxed sets of CDs. Luckily, most material is also available on single CDs, so you can pick and choose your favorite songs: *The Voice of Jazz: The Complete Recordings 1933–40* (Affinity, 8 CDs)—all the Columbia recordings; *The Complete Original American Decca Recordings* (MCA, 2 CDs) collects her work 1944–50, much of it more popular song than jazz, but just as ravishing; *The Complete Billie Holiday on Verve* (Verve, 10 CDs) is all her studio work and concert performances recorded by Verve between 1945 and her death in 1959.

Strange Fruit

"Scent of magnolia sweet and fresh, Then the sudden smell of burning flesh." Alongside her usual songs documenting unrequited love and no-good lovers, Billie Holiday's *Strange Fruit*—a graphic description of a lynching in the Deep South—stands out for its in-your-face anti-racist politics. The powerful song—written by Lewis Allen—was an unlikely hit for Holiday in 1939 and gained her a liberal, intellectual (and white) audience she might otherwise not have attracted. But it was atypical in her repertoire, as if her own particular brand of personal horror was more than enough to be going on with.

1955 In Alabama, Rosa Parks defies the segregation laws and refuses to give up her seat on a bus to a white man.

1958 The American Express credit card is launched.

1959 Italian director, Federico Fellini's "scandalous" film *La Dolce Vita* arrives in the U.S.

Diana Ross's portrayal in *Lady Sings the Blues* (1972) overemphasized the harsher side of Lady Day's life.

used that voice to magnificent effect on material that looked on the face of it less than promising. Faced with Tin Pan Alley lyrics that do not bear close inspection, she would rework a song into a personal testimony. If the melody wasn't right, she would depart from it, or abandon it altogether, drawing out an emotional and melodic beauty from what was otherwise trivial or banal.

On stage, she presented no show, merely coming on, singing—her head at a slight, defiant tilt—taking the applause and leaving. There was no showmanship, no act, yet she was a real actress, who drew on her own feelings and conveyed them with an honest directness to the audience. It was some show.

Another scene from *Lady Sings the Blues*: on tour in the early days.

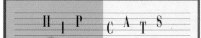

HIP CATS

As a singer, Billie Holiday had no regular backup group, but throughout her life played with musicians from the best bands, notably those of Benny Goodman, Count Basie, and Artie Shaw, briefly her lover. Her ideal partner was Lester Young, but trumpeter **Roy Eldridge** *(1911–89) ran a close second for his relaxed sensitivity and effortless ability in the higher registers. Pianist* **Teddy Wilson** *(1912–86) was Holiday's musical director; by himself, he was sometimes accused of being a mere cocktail-bar pianist, but with Holiday he was a sympathetic and supportive accompanist who did much to lift her voice.*

1929 In Paris, Salvador Dali exhibits his surrealist paintings for the first time.

1930 Soccer's first World Cup tournament takes place in Uruguay and is won by the host country.

1932 The neutron, a new subatomic particle, is discovered.

1928~1941
A Left Hand Like God
Boogie Woogie

It inspired some of Piet Mondrian's most energetic paintings, started a famous record label, and sent the troops off to war urged on by a certain bugle boy from Company B, but the mother and father of boogie woogie music was that usual suspect: sex. Robert "Fud" Shaw, an early exponent, stated: "When you listen to what I'm playing, you got to see in your mind all them girls out there swinging their butts and getting the mens excited. Otherwise you ain't got the music rightly understood ... That's what this music is for."

Meade "Lux" Lewis,
a boogie-woogie
heavyweight in every way.

Boogie woogie started as a good-time, low-down dance music played by blues pianists in bars and rent parties. Pine Top's *Boogie Woogie*—written in 1928 by *Pine Top SMITH* (1904–29) and printed with instructions for the dance steps on top of the score—set the music's style. While the right hand pounded out the melody with big block chords and fast runs, the left hand played a driving, repetitive eight notes to the bar—a walking bass line with notes an octave apart moving crabwise up and down the keyboard, or with pairs of notes with the top one shifting up or down, or similar repetitive patterns. The style varied from player to player, and confusingly, boogie woogie, blues, and stride styles often blurred at their edges—

Unfortunate deaths

Could be the start of a long-running series, because jazz is full of them, but few can beat poor young Pine Top Smith, accidentally shot at the age of 25 during a brawl at a Masonic Lodge where he was performing. Consider also legendary blues singer Robert Johnson (1911–38), who was poisoned with whisky by the cheated husband whose wife he was seeing at the time. Music sure is a dangerous game.

but whoever played what, boogie woogie was always eight notes to the bar, stride was four. To play boogie-woogie required considerable concentration, dexterity, and a left hand like God.

The music's heyday was in the 1920s, when rent parties and honky-tonks flourished, but the Depression swept all that away, and boogie woogie disappeared

1934 The cheeseburger, served for the first time by Carl Kaelen at his burger bar in Louisville, Kentucky, is an instant success.

1939 Brazilian singer, dancer, and actress Carmen Miranda appears in the extraordinary "fruit basket" headdresses that come to be her trademark.

1940 Benjamin O. Davis, Sr., becomes the first black general in the U.S. army.

ALL THAT JAZZ

ALBERT AMMONS— *Albert Ammons 1936–1939* (Classics)
PETE JOHNSON—*Pete Johnson 1938–1939* and *1939–1941* (both on Classics)
MEADE LUX LEWIS— *Meade Lux Lewis 1927–1939* and *1939–1941* (both on Classics)
BOOGIE WOOGIE— *Blue Boogie* (Blue Note)—a compilation of piano jazz styles.

---

from view. Until December 23, 1938, when record producer and entrepreneur *John* HAMMOND (1910–87)— responsible for, among many others, Billie Holiday— promoted a concert at Carnegie Hall entitled From Spirituals to Swing. He searched out *Albert AMMONS* (1907–49) and *Meade "Lux" LEWIS* (1905–64), both working as taxi drivers in Chicago, joined them with *Pete JOHNSON* (1904–67) from Kansas City, and put them all on stage. They played up a storm, and then an even bigger storm the following year when, as the Boogie Woogie Trio, accompanied by singer *Big Joe TURNER* (1911–85), they played a residency at Café Society in New York. The boogie-woogie boom was born, sweeping all before it with its infectious eight-to-the-bar. Early masters of the art such as *Jimmy YANCEY* (*c.*1894–1951) were rediscovered, and lots of people made lots of money—notably the Andrews Sisters with their accursed bugle boy. Then the traumas of war led to a demand for smoother sounds, like those of Glenn Miller, more "In the Mood" for the times. But it was good fun while it lasted.

Blue Note Records

The most famous of all jazz labels was formed as a direct result of the Spirituals to Swing concert. In the audience was Alfred Lion (1908–87), a refugee from Nazi Germany. So enthused was he by the three boogie-woogie pianists, he set up Blue Note Records and on January 6, 1939, recorded Ammons and Lewis in four solos each and two duets. Only fifty 78-rpm disks of the session were made, but soon the label had its first hit with Sidney Bechet's version of *Summertime*. Lion was joined by fellow refugee Francis Wolff, and after a brief break during the war the label made its name with an impressive roster of early jazz, swing, and later bop. What distinguished the label, which survives to this day, was its attention to recording quality—safe in the hands of engineer Rudy Van Gelder after 1953—and the style of its record sleeves, designed and often photographed by graphic designer Reid Miles. For many, Blue Note is the epitome of jazz chic.

Twisting and turning to the irresistible boogie-woogie beat.

1934 In Louisiana, blues singer Leadbelly is released from jail after writing a song to the governor begging for a pardon.

1936 The first Butlins Holiday Camp opens in Skegness, Lincolnshire.

1937 The insecticide DDT is invented by Swiss scientist Paul Müller.

1934~1954

Hot Jazz

Django Reinhardt and Stéphane Grappelli

A night on the town for Stéphane Grappelli. In later life he would become more unbuttoned.

Other than the U.S., the country in which jazz put down its strongest roots was France. With a tradition of nightclubs and cabaret, as well as a degree of racial tolerance, France was more receptive to the brash new music than, say, hidebound Britain. In 1932 a group of jazz fans in Paris formed Europe's first jazz club, the Hot Club de France, under the presidency of writer and critic Hugues Panassié. At first it was just chat and records, but in 1934 the club decided to promote its own jazz quintet. One of the three guitarists was Django REINHARDT (1910–53); the violinist was Stéphane GRAPPELLI (1908–97).

The two could not have been more different. Grappelli was a middle-class Parisian with classical training. Reinhardt was born a gypsy in Belgium and was entirely self-taught. Grappelli was urbane and easy; Reinhardt was difficult, undisciplined, unpredictable, but also an innovator of genius. At times his style could be cloyingly romantic, but at his best he was a stunning performer and composer with superb technical skill, despite a left hand crippled in a caravan fire when he

was 18. At a time when big bands were everything, the Quintette du Hot Club de France— ignited by the rapport between its two main soloists—was a huge success.

The best work of the quintet was during the 1930s.

Jazz criticism

While those who can do, those who can't write criticism. And since Americans can, Europeans write. Not strictly true, but by the mid-1920s jazz criticism was thriving in Europe. The first books—Robert Goffin's *Aux frontières du jazz* (1932) and Panassié's *Le jazz hot* (1934)— both appeared in Europe, as did the first jazz magazine, Panassié's *Jazz hot* in 1935. In America, various magazines had run features on the music from the 1920s on. Then in 1934 a trade paper for dance-band musicians, *Down Beat*, was founded, which soon turned itself over entirely to jazz.

1938 Orson Welles broadcasts *War of the Worlds,* his radio science-fiction drama about Martian invasion, and

1951 The Festival of Britain takes place on London's South Bank in celebration of the nation's art, architecture, design, and industry.

1953 United States authorities refuse Charlie Chaplin re-entry to the country, pending allegations of Communist activities

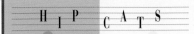

HIP CATS

There are legions of Reinhardt copyists, notably fellow gypsy **Bireli Lagrene** *(b.1966) and, in a milder way, British-born* **Martin Taylor** *(b.1956), one of Grappelli's later and best accompanists. Grappelli has few direct imitators, but debts are owed by electric violinist* **Jean-Luc Ponty** *(b.1942), who has recorded with everyone from John McLaughlin to Frank Zappa, and* **Didier Lockwood** *(b.1956).*

new bop music, and took up the electric guitar, but it never sounded quite the same again. Grappelli fell out of favor, but enjoyed a renaissance during the 1960s, which saw him play with everyone from electric violinist Jean-Luc Ponty to classical maestro Yehudi Menuhin,

The "Gypsy Guitarist" Django Reinhardt in a characteristic playing pose.

with little apparent damage endured by either side. Like a good wine, he matured with age, throwing aside his classical training and letting his emotions show through at last.

The outbreak of war in 1939 split the initial members: Grappelli remained in exile in London while Reinhardt and the rest performed in occupied Europe. After the war, Reinhardt reformed the quintet with other members, tried to cope with the

ALL THAT JAZZ

DJANGO REINHARDT—Classics is bringing out all the Reinhardt material, with 11 volumes issued to date, covering 1934–46. *Swing From Paris* (ASV) contains much fine pre-war material from 1938–39. **STÉPHANE GRAPPELLI**—*Grappelli Story* (Verve, 2 CDs) is a compilation of Grappelli music 1938–92; *Reunion* (Linn) is a fine 1993 duo with guitarist Martin Taylor. For violin pyrotechnics, try *Violin Summit* (Saba), or *Stéphane Grappelli/Jean-Luc Ponty* (Accord) from 1972–73.

The Hot Club Quintet recording in London, including Reinhardt (central of the three guitarists) and Grappelli.

1944 Frederick D. Patterson founds the United Negro College Fund.

1945 In Kansas, car stickers appear for the first time.

1946 The world's skimpiest swimsuit, the "bikini" designed by Louis Réard, explodes onto the fashion scene.

1940~1950
New Noise at Minton's
The Birth of Bop

Stylish Dizzy Gillespie with trademark beret: a jazz hipster.

While the world went to war, jazz stayed behind and staged a revolution. Like all revolutions, it began with a few outbursts by a dedicated sect of hotshots, but soon it spread like wildfire and everyone was involved, whether they liked it not. Most did not, and even the genial Louis Armstrong said that the new music, known as bop, had "no melody to remember and no beat to dance to." Unlike swing, which embraced its audience with open arms, bop appeared to turn its back on them. Eventually the revolutionaries won, and everyone embraced everyone else, but then, as with all revolutions, they became the new establishment.

T he seeds of this revolution were born in Minton's Playhouse in Harlem, opened by saxophonist Henry Minton in 1938. When bandleader Teddy Hill took it over in 1940, he set up regular Monday night jam sessions at which visiting musicians, notably trumpeter *Dizzy GILLESPIE* (1917–93) and saxophonist *Charlie PARKER* (1920–55), could blow with the house band, which included pianist *Thelonious MONK* (1917–82) and drummer *Kenny CLARKE* (1914–85).

The war
The onset of war in 1941 hit big bands hard, with many musicians called up to fight. A shortage of shellac restricted record production, and the American Federation of Musicians imposed a recording ban in protest at unlicensed broadcasting of records. Singers, unaffected by the ban, grabbed much of the market by providing the sentimental lyrics a stressed-out population demanded. One exception to the ban was recordings made as part of the war effort; more than 900 records were released on V (victory) disks exclusively for distribution to U.S. military personnel. A by-product of the ban was that the early days of bop went completely unrecorded, until the music burst onto an unsuspecting public during 1944. America, however, had it easy. In occupied Europe, both Nazis and Soviets considered jazz a degenerate music. Jazz clubs were closed, and many musicians ended their lives in concentration camps.

1947 Brothers Leonard and Phil Chess form the recording label Aristocrat (later renamed Chess Records), to give black singers a chance to record urban blues.

1948 The Kinsey Report on sexuality in the human male is published in the U.S.

1949 George Orwell's futuristic novel *Nineteen Eighty-Four* is published.

New New Orleans

Every action is met with an equal and opposite reaction. And so it was with bop, in reaction to which there was a revival in New Orleans jazz—and several players' careers, notably trumpeter Bunk Johnson. The revivalist movement was, however, fundamentally reactionary, and much of the music was soon preserved in aspic. But Europe reveled in this time warp, and "trad" bands enjoyed great success in Britain during the 1950s. And still do today, sadly.

Collectively, and individually, they turned their back on the simplicities and certainties of swing and began to develop a far more complex music. More about Gillespie, Parker, and Monk later.

The new music was built around small groups of four or five musicians, rather than the uneconomic big swing bands now decimated by conscription—but it retained the basic 12-bar blues and 32-bar popular song formats used by swing. Where it differed was in harmony, rhythm, and structure. Harmonically, bop was more complex, improvising over modified chords with many notes added, and altering and substituting those chords on a regular, rapid basis. Rhythmically, swing's basic four-beat bar was now stated by the double bass, with the drummer using the ride cymbal and hi-hat to place accents in unpredictable places. Kenny Clarke was a master at this, using a light touch to push and pull the beat toward a multilayered pulse, upping the tension considerably. Structurally, bop did away with the organized swing charts; most pieces opened and closed with a unison statement of the

Bop or what?

Be-bop or re-bop music got its name either from the nonsense words used by singers on a two-note descending phrase, when they made words up rather than sing proper lyrics, or from the sound made by the offbeat accents of the new music. Musicians disliked the term at the time, but be-bop, or bop, was there to stay.

theme, leaving plenty of space in between for the virtuoso soloists to improvise over those complex chords.

Add all these elements together, and speed it up—for bop was never slow—and you have a music that turned the jazz world upside down.

The Three Deuces Club on 52d Street in New York became another important venue for the new be-bop style that hit Harlem in the 1940s.

1942 The musical biopic *Yankee Doodle Dandy* (1942) opens starring James Cagney as George M. Cohan, the actor, singer, dancer, and playwright who dominated American theater in the early 20th century.

1943 Irish coffee is introduced by chef Joe Sheridan and served at Shannon Airport, Ireland, to passengers from the Pan Am flying boat service.

1947 U.S. Air Force captain Chuck Yeager, in an experimental X-1 rocket plane, becomes the first person to travel faster than the speed of sound.

1941~1955

Bird Flies
Charlie Parker

Charlie Parker with Strings, not one of Bird's more successful outings.

If Armstrong elevated jazz from entertainment to an art form, Charlie PARKER *(1920–55) placed it firmly in the avant-garde. For jazz critic (and famous poet) Philip Larkin, Parker stood alongside Ezra Pound and Pablo Picasso as one of the high priests of modernism, playing a supremely ugly music that had gone "from Lascaux to Jackson Pollock in fifty years." Larkin strongly disapproved of this deviation from his beloved Stone Age jazz, but few now share his criticisms of jazz's finest modernist, indeed its finest musician.*

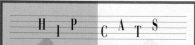

Parker worked with all the finest bop musicians, including trumpeters **Dizzy Gillespie** *(1917–93), bass player* **Charles Mingus** *(1922–79), and pianists* **Thelonious Monk** *(1917–82) and* **Bud Powell** *(1924–66). One of his key quintets included the young* **Miles Davis** *(1926–91) on trumpet; drummer* **Max Roach** *(b.1925), a disciple of* **Kenny Clarke**, *who propelled the music with a headlong surge of cross-rhythms; pianist* **Duke Jordan** *(b.1922), who had assimilated the bop techniques of Bud Powell; and bassist* **Tommy Potter** *(1918–88).* **J. J. Johnson** *(b.1924) showed how even the ungainly trombone could cope with the requirements of fast bop.*

Charlie Parker was a compulsive in everything he did, consuming vast amounts of drink, drugs, food, women, and music. But by the time his body eventually gave up the struggle, he had transformed jazz by consuming its entire history and reinventing it afresh. Not by himself, for others developed bop music with him, but without his brilliance the future of jazz would have sounded very different.

Parker's skill lay in his speed of thought and fingering, his fertile mind and agile fingers enabling him to construct perfect solos at great speed and for considerable lengths of time. Soaring across the bar lines, he developed solos over complex chord changes that were harmonically advanced but which sounded completely natural. He paused in unexpected places,

1951 Christian organizations in the U.S. denounce J.D. Salinger's first novel, *A Catcher in the Rye*. Elsewhere, the novel has many supporters.

1954 Roger Bannister breaks the four-minute mile record, passing the line at 3 minutes 59.4 seconds.

1955 Chuck Berry has a top-ten hit with his first single, "Maybelline."

The lifestyle

Long before rock musicians made fools of themselves by taking copious amounts of drugs, jazz musicians were doing it to the extreme. Long hours, late nights, grueling schedules, and an erratic lifestyle led inevitably to drugs—cocaine and marijuana in the '20s and '30s, and heroin in the 1940s. Hard drugs fueled and later exhausted Parker (who often had his horn in hock to pay for his next fix), pickled Chet Baker for life, and ate most of Billie Holiday's earnings—appallingly, she was arrested for narcotics possession on her deathbed. Name a famous young musician in the 1940s or 1950s, and you are probably naming an addict.

added emphasis where least expected, and changed speed as if on a whim, but each time out came the perfect solo, delivered with a light, bouncy touch and a tone that sliced through butter.

In everything Parker did, he gave the impression that it was all so childishly easy—the phrase "effortless superiority" was coined for him—but an older generation of musicians was appalled that their well-honed skills were no longer up to the task, and struggled to keep up. Parker, meanwhile, flew on ahead. By the end of his life, he was working with strings and

> ### Relaxin' at Camarillo
>
> Not a vacation resort, or a comfortable bar on a beach somewhere, but the state hospital outside Los Angeles where Charlie Parker spent six months in 1947–48 for an alcohol and heroin-induced breakdown, evident after he ignited his hotel bed and walked naked throught the streets. In the hospital, he received electric shock treatment. Once out, he wrote a relaxed little tune about it all.

expressing interest in the music of Varèse and Stravinsky. His legacy is immense, for unlike most jazz pioneers, who influenced succeeding performers of the same instrument, Parker's influence is felt by jazz musicians of every ilk.

A slimline Parker—modeling for every later saxophonist.

> ### ALL THAT JAZZ
>
> *The Charlie Parker Story* (Savoy): early recordings from 1945; *Charlie Parker on Dial: The Complete Recordings* (Spotlite/Dial, 4 CDs): 1945–47 recordings from East and West coasts; *Bird: The Complete Charlie Parker on Verve* (Verve, 10 CDs): sessions from 1946–52, also available as numerous individual disks; *The Quintet/Jazz at Massey Hall* (OJC): a live set from Toronto in 1953.

1946 London's first postwar bananas go on sale at Covent Garden Market.

1947 The Dead Sea Scrolls are discovered in Jordan by a shepherd looking for a lost sheep.

1955 In New York, the League of Decency forces a giant poster of Marilyn Monroe with her skirts billowing, an advertisement for the film *The Seven Year Itch*, to be removed.

1943~1993

Cubana Be, Cubana Bop
Dizzy Gillespie

Dizzy's one-time employer, the showman Cab Calloway.

If Parker was the high priest of bop, Dizzy GILLESPIE (1917–93) was its master of ceremonies. An extrovert showman, whose dizzy antics on stage gave him his nickname (he was christened John Birks Gillespie), he set bop alight with pyrotechnic displays of pure invention. Even his trumpet was special: when someone fell on it at a party in 1953 and bent the horn to a racy angle, Gillespie had another one made just the same, because "I hear the sound quicker that way."

Latin Jazz

Gillespie wasn't the first to bring Latin music into jazz—in 1941 an Afro-Latin big band led by Machito (1912–84) was making a big noise in New York—but he had always been interested in the music and formed his own Latin big band in 1947. The band was built around the conga player Chano Pozo (1915–48) and produced such masterpieces as *Manteca* and *Cubana Be, Cubana Bop*, merging the rhythms of Cuban drumming with the harmonies of bop into cubop. Later in his career he worked with Machito and continued to explore the fertile ground of Latin jazz.

Like many bop musicians, Gillespie emerged out of the swing era, playing first with the Teddy Hill Band—replacing his idol Roy Eldridge—and then in the Hi Di Hi show band of *Cab CALLOWAY* (1907–94). That suited his over-the-top personality, but musically it was restricting, so he veered toward the bop pioneers, gigging after hours at Minton's from 1941. With bassist *Oscar PETTIFORD* (1922–60) he formed in 1943 the first-ever bop band to play in a mainstream New York club, the Onyx on 52d Street, and, most importantly, he played in 1944 on the first-ever bop recordings, under the leadership of Coleman Hawkins.

His partnership with Parker ensures Gillespie's status: Parker had the great ideas, Gillespie fleshed them out and taught other musicians how to build on

1961 Cuban exiles, trained and armed by the U.S., attempt to invade Cuba's "Bay of Pigs" and overthrow Castro.

1962 Cigar smokers are badly hit by the American ban on all trade with Cuba.

1967 Queen of Soul Aretha Franklin has four top-ten hits; *Respect* is adopted as an anthem for black and feminist movements.

HIP CATS

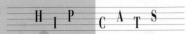

*Gillespie started out as an admirer of trumpeter **Roy Eldridge** (1911–89), who had played with Fletcher Henderson's Big Band and accompanied Billie Holiday, but managed to fit well into the new landscape of bop. In their turn, trumpeters **Howard McGhee** (1918–87) and **Fats Navarro** (1923–50) both admired Gillespie, McGhee playing on some of Parker's finest dates, while many consider Navarro to be the most complete of all bop trumpeters: more assertive than Miles Davis, better organized than McGhee, less flamboyant than Gillespie. **Jon Faddis** (b.1953) and Cuban-born **Arturo Sandoval** (b.1949)—trumpet pyrotechnicians both—are Gillespie's natural heirs.*

WHITE HOUSE DIZZY

In retrospect, it is easy to dismiss Gillespie as a showman, a jovial man with a funny trumpet and bulging cheeks who clowned around on stage. But this man also fought for jazz to be recognized as a major art form, and was a dedicated anti-racist campaigner, even threatening to run for president in 1980. True to form, he said that if elected he would rename the White House the Blues House and make Miles Davis head of the CIA. Shame he didn't run, really.

ALL THAT JAZZ

DIZZY GILLESPIE—*Groovin' High* (Savoy): essential bop sessions from 1945–46; *The Complete RCA Victor Recordings* (RCA Bluebird, 2 CDs): small and big band recordings from swing to bop, 1937–49, including the Latin big band with Chano Pozo; *Birks Works* (Verve, 2 CDs): the cultural ambassador's working band, 1956–57.
COLEMAN HAWKINS—*Rainbow Mist* (Delmark): the first-ever bop recordings, February 1944.

them. Many famous bop compositions—*Groovin' High, Night in Tunisia, Salt Peanuts*—are by Gillespie, and his hipster style of beret, shades, and goatee defined what modern jazz should wear. Then Gillespie left Parker to his wayward devices and set up the first bop big band in 1945. It was a financial disaster, but in 1946 he tried again, introducing Latin rhythms and gaining a wide audience for bop. In the 1950s he became a jazz ambassador, touring the world for the U.S. State Department and adopting the role of jazz's elder statesman. Later he led the United Nations band on grueling city-a-night tours.

His solos often went into orbit—helped by pointing them in the right direction.

1946 Dr. Benjamin Spock's world-famous *The Commonsense Book of Baby and Childcare* is published.

1947 Jackie Robinson is invited to join the Brooklyn Dodgers. This marks the breaking of the color barrier in major-league baseball.

1951 Transcontinental television is inaugurated with an address by President Truman on the Japanese Peace Treaty Conference in San Francisco.

1942~1965

Bouncing with Bud
Bud Powell

With all the urgency of Parker's alto sax and the fire of Gillespie's trumpet, Bud POWELL (1924–66) gave the piano a bop language of its own. His right hand punched out fast, melodic lines of notes that sounded more like what came from a harsh-toned saxophone than a piano. In contrast, his left hand restricted itself to irregularly spaced, dissonant chords, punctuation marks in the right-hand stream of consciousness. Put the two together, and Powell rewrote the piano book.

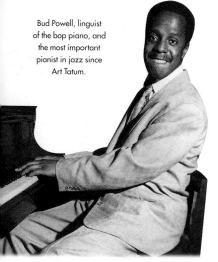

Bud Powell, linguist of the bop piano, and the most important pianist in jazz since Art Tatum.

> ### ALL THAT JAZZ
>
> **BUD POWELL**—*The Complete Bud Powell on Verve* (Verve, 5 CDs); *The Amazing Bud Powell* (Blue Note, two volumes): volume two includes *The Glass Enclosure.*
>
> **NAT KING COLE**—*The Best of the Nat King Cole Trio* (Capitol): with guitar and bass.
>
> **ERROL GARNER**—*The Original Misty* (Mercury), including his most famous composition; *Concert by the Sea* (Columbia): a live set from 1955 and one of the biggest-selling jazz records of all time.
>
> **OSCAR PETERSON**—*Verve Jazz Masters: Oscar Peterson* (Verve): in trio and other formats 1952–61; *Night Train* (Verve): a 1962 quartet set with bass, drums, and vibes; *The Trio* (Verve): a 1973 trio set with the guitar of Joe Pass and the bass of Danish maestro Niels-Henning Ørsted Pedersen.

E ven today, Powell's rapid, and unpredictable melodies, delivered with a brittle, precise touch, continue to amaze. His right-hand phrases consist sometimes of merely a few flurries of notes, or stride over the bars forever; yet despite the torrent of his ideas and the all-around percussive attack, there is a sparseness about his work in contrast to the lushness of an Art Tatum. And he used that sparseness to great effect, working in new melodic ideas and harmonies, and exploring different ways to link the two hands together.

His achievement is all the more incredible set against his personal history.

1956 Clairol hair-coloring advertisements ask, "Does she or doesn't she?"

1962 The Beatles leap to success with their first single, *Love Me Do.*

1964 In London, three women are found guilty of indecency for wearing topless dresses.

In 1945 he was hospitalized, allegedly as a result of a head injury following a racial assault, and from then on suffered recurring bouts of mental illness, for which he received electroshock treatment in 1951–52. He struggled on, often heavily tranquilized, and spent considerable time in sanatoriums—*The Glass Enclosure*, written in 1953, is his musical impression of asylum life. He took up residence in Paris in 1959, but was by now drinking heavily. He also contracted tuberculosis. Playing more erratically than ever, he returned to New York in 1964, made one final, disastrous appearance at Carnegie Hall in 1965, and then abandoned music altogether. At his funeral in August 1966, more than five thousand people lined the streets of Harlem to pay their last respects. A vulnerable man with an invulnerable touch.

Oscar Peterson, one of the most prolific jazz recording artists, with his trio. Peterson never fails to amaze for his sheer musicianship and effusive performances. Classic trio jazz in every respect.

Nat King Cole (right) before his crooning career began.

The classic jazz trio

Piano, double bass, and drums: the classic jazz group of all time. Yet strangely the format took time to get established, as the stride and blues pianists were in the main solo men; and when it did, guitar rather than drums provided the rhythm. Nat King Cole (1917–65)—now better known as a crooner—was one of the first in the ring, producing some fine trio work after 1937, the accompaniment highlighting his flowing, cleanly articulated style. Art Tatum copied the guitar/bass instrumentation in 1943, but it was Errol Garner (1921–77), a swooningly romantic player, who first worked with bass and drums, establishing his trio in 1944. The pianist who has made the trio format his own is Oscar Peterson (b.1925), a black Canadian with classical training and supreme technical skills whose trios have used both guitarists and drummers. Peterson can be cloyingly sweet, and his technique can sometimes overwhelm his material, but at his best, with both hands flying, he is mesmerizing.

1945 *Ebony* magazine is founded in the U.S., by Chicago publisher John H. Johnson.

1946 50,000 "G.I. brides" make their journey from Britain to start new lives with their sweethearts in the U.S.

1947 The House Un-American Activities Committee begins to investigate the Communist influence within the film industry. Ten motion-picture professionals are blacklisted for supposed Communist connections.

1945~1960

Dinosaurs Live On
Postwar Big Bands

After the double whammy of war and bop, the big bands were reeling. Their traveling circus was coming to an end, and even the bandleaders tired of trotting out signature tunes night after night— Shaw's Begin the Beguine *and Goodman's* Stompin' at the Savoy *palled at their millionth performance. Audiences, of course, still demanded that favorite song one more time, but the line from success through repetition to cliché was direct and painfully quick. By 1945 it looked as if all these dinosaurs had had their day.*

The ebullient Lionel Hampton, another survivor from the big band era.

Jazz at the Philharmonic

The idea of a touring road show of jazz stars began with impresario Norman Granz, who staged a charity concert at the Philharmonic Auditorium in L.A. in July 1944. In 1945, the first JATP show toured a few U.S. cities, and by the 1950s, it consisted of worldwide performances and lasted for seven months a year. The format was part concert, part jam session, and the quantity of star names often rated more than the quality of the music, but JATP brought jazz to an audience of millions.

But like real dinosaurs, the big bands didn't die out, but evolved into new life forms—although some were preserved in aspic, awaiting a Spielbergian revival in jazz's Jurassic Park. *Stan* KENTON (1912–79) updated his 1941 hit *Artistry in Rhythm* and, with the "progressive jazz" tag, got together a band with ten brass players in 1947 and embraced dissonance in a big way. It was nothing if not noisy. Spurred on by its success, he then went completely over the top, and in 1950–52 ran the 43-piece Innovations in Modern Music Orchestra, which included 16 string players and mixed classical music, the avant-garde, jazz soloing, and Ellingtonian arrangements. Pretentious, or what?

1948 Mahatma Gandhi is assassinated by a nationalist extremist following the partition of British Imperial India into India and Pakistan.

1957 Actress Jean Seberg catches fire during filming of the burning-at-the-stake sequence in *Saint Joan.*

1960 The laser beam is developed by Hughes Research Laboratories in the U.S.

Woody HERMAN (1913–87) took another route. His "Band That Plays the Blues" had had a huge hit in the 1930s with *Woodchopper's Ball*, but in the 1940s he updated its sound with arrangements by the hugely talented *Neal HEFTI* (b.1922) and others. The First Herd—as his band was known—was good, the Second Herd, magnificent. Hidden within were four saxophonists—tenors *Stan GETZ* (1927–91), *Zoot SIMS* (1925–85), and *Herbie STEWARD* (b.1926), and baritone *Serge CHALOFF* (1923–57)—known as the Four Brothers, whose distinctive, smooth voicings gave the band a modern edge. Third and Fourth Herds followed, although during their annual breaks, non-numerical Swinging, Thundering, and Anglo-American Herds took to the road in their stead.

Meanwhile, much-loved institutions bided their time and rode out the evolutionary storm. Count Basie brought in new musicians and used the ubiquitous Neal Hefti to arrange new material. *The Atomic Mr. Basie* ($e = mc^2 =$ Count Basie Orchestra plus Neal Hefti Arrangements!) was a modern classic in its cold-war, atom bomb cover, but the music inside was still recognizably Basie. Likewise, Duke Ellington continued to churn out suites and tour the world, his band still packed with the finest in jazz. In the midst of huge change, some things just didn't need to change that much at all, while some people never wanted any change in the first place.

ALL THAT JAZZ

COUNT BASIE—*The Complete Atomic Mr. Basie* (Roulette): a cold war classic from 1957.
WOODY HERMAN—*At the Woodchoppers Ball* (ASV); *Keeper of the Flame* (Capitol): the Second Herd's finest.
STAN KENTON—*City of Glass* (Capitol): progressive jazz from 1947–53; *The Innovations Orchestra* (Capitol); *New Concepts of Artistry in Rhythm* (Capitol): more prog jazz from 1952.
JATP—*JATP in London,* 1969 (Pablo); *JATP at the Montreux Festival,* 1975 (Pablo).

Woody Herman, super-trooper of the big-band touring circuit.

1947 The Antoinette Perry, or "Tony" awards are established for outstanding contributions to American theater.

1948 Wurlitzer's flashiest jukebox—the Wurlitzer 1100—becomes a big hit in bars and clubs worldwide.

1952 The Immigration and Naturalization Act is passed, removing the last racial and ethnic barriers to naturalization.

1947~1982

'Round Midnight
Thelonious Monk

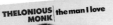

Monk—hat and beard at the piano, one of the renowned jazz eccentrics.

Thelonious Sphere MONK (1917–82)—Melodious Thunk, as dubbed by his wife—is by any account a name to conjure with and a man to listen to. He played stop-start music on the piano, with clusters of jarring notes and long, unexpected pauses. A Heath-Robinson sort of music, with strange attachments and bits and pieces that don't seem to go anywhere, but work perfectly well even if you can't quite see how or why. An ungainly music, yet in its quirky, meticulous, and audacious way, a near-perfect music of compelling, idiosyncratic beauty.

Monk wasn't really interested in music until his twenties, but then made up for lost time, and in 1940 was in the house band at Minton's, the powerhouse of bop. He was a loner, and preferred to visit the club out of hours so that he could practice alone. He made his first visit to a recording studio in 1944, and in the same year his most famous tune, 'Round Midnight, was recorded by trumpeter *Cootie WILLIAMS* (1911–85), one of Duke Ellington's men. In 1947, at the age of 30, he made his first recordings

On Monk's music

If you missed a chord change, it was "like falling into an empty elevator shaft."—John Coltrane. His music was full of surprises, "like missing the bottom step in the dark."—Whitney Balliett, *New Yorker* critic.

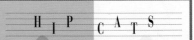

HIP CATS

*Monk played with many of jazz's finest musicians, including Art Blakey, Miles Davis, Sonny Rollins, and John Coltrane (about all of whom, more later). One of his most enduring partnerships was with saxophonist **Charlie Rouse** (1924–88), who was with him from 1959 to 1970. Rouse had a distinctive nasal tone and a choppy, rhythmic style, both of which suited Monk's idiosyncratic playing. It is not surprising that few piano players have followed Monk who was a total original. But for his angular, rhythmic belligerence, the British pianist **Stan Tracey** (b.1926) comes close, despite his obvious debt to Ellington.*

1967 The first quartz wristwatch is launched by Seiko.

1973 Glam Rock, spearheaded by David Bowie and his Ziggy Stardust tour, reaches its height.

1976 Concorde offers its first scheduled supersonic commercial service.

Thelonious Monk in earlier life: his unique compositions have had a big impact on the development of modern jazz.

under his own name for Blue Note records, entitled *Genius of Modern Jazz*, and his style was set for life.

GENIUS

At this point I would remind you of Adams's Rules of Jazz, the one which advises that "genius" should be used only sparingly. But with Monk the cap fits. Blue Note recognized it, but not many others agreed, and it wasn't until he began to record for Prestige in 1955 that he gained wider recognition. The albums *Brilliant Corners* and *Monk's Music* were masterpieces, as were his performances with tenor saxophonist *John COLTRANE* (1926–67) in 1957, and Monk was now in demand—so much so that in 1964 he made the cover of *Time* magazine: rare recognition for a jazz musician. He toured the world, but eventually he was merely going through his paces, so in 1971, he all but retired. Whatever jazz you listen to, you can't now avoid Monk. *'Round Midnight*; *Blue Monk*; *Well You Needn't*; *Straight, No Chaser*; *Misterioso*: these and more of his compositions form the essential backbone of so much modern jazz. A main man, totally, and once heard never to be forgotten. In a word, essential.

Andrew Hill

Room for author indulgence at this point, for if Chicago-born pianist Andrew Hill (b. 1937) doesn't get a look-in here, there's nowhere else to place him. Like Monk, Hill is unclassifiable. His main claim to fame is as leader on a series of outstanding records for Blue Note during the 1960s, using Monklike figures as the basis for knotty, convoluted improvisations that sounded like nothing else before—"Monk with wings" is as good a description as any. By the end of the decade he was playing increasingly freestyle, but then dropped from view as rock held sway. On his return in the mid-1970s, he honed his considerable technique into solo performances, playing with controlled intensity. To my mind (says the author, making a rare personal appearance in the text), one of the greatest of jazz pianists, but not everyone agrees with me!

1948 In the U.S. a judge rules that it is illegal for homeowners to refuse to sell to black buyers.

1949 The first training shoe is launched by German sports manufacturer Addas (later renamed Adidas).

1950 Texan elevator attendants have their noses put out of joint as Otis, in Dallas, installs the first passenger elevator with automatic doors.

1948~1959

Jazz Cools Down
The Birth of the Cool

Newton's Third Law comes into play here once again. We've already noted one reaction to all-conquering bop—the retrogressive movement that was the New Orleans revival—but there was also a reaction of more long-lasting importance, a move forward, a reaction to the hot of bop with the cool of, obviously enough, Cool. And in at the birth of Cool was trumpeter supreme Miles DAVIS (1926–91).

The Birth of the Cool: seminal arrangements for an all-star group.

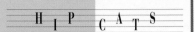
W e're going to encounter Miles many more times in these pages, but in 1948 he was fresh out of Charlie Parker's band and hanging around with like-minded ex-Parker people looking for new sounds to play. Also looking around were members of the disbanded Claude Thornhill band—renowned for its advanced arrangements and interesting instrumentation, including tubas and French horns—notably composer and baritone saxophonist *Gerry MULLIGAN* (1927–96) and arranger *Gil EVANS* (1912–88), who both wanted to get "a good little rehearsal band together: something to write for." With Davis, they rejected the rip-roaring approach of bop in favor of a contemplative, ethereal music, which owed much to the cooler approach of Lester Young. Together they started to flesh out some ideas for a nonet—nine musicians, the smallest number which could best replicate the rich sound of the (much bigger) Thornhill band.

1953 Lita Rosa becomes the first woman to have a number-one hit on the U.K. charts with *How Much Is That Doggy in the Window?*

1954 In Britain rationing ends, and ration books are burnt across the U.K. The last items to come off rationing are bacon and sugar.

1959 A fire breaks out in the Cinecittà studios in Rome, destroying the sets for director Carmine Gallone's *Carthage in Flames.*

This band-in-progress was still ill-prepared when it was hired for a two-week residency in September 1948 at New York's Royal Roost Club. It was billed as "The Miles Davis Band: arrangements by Gerry Mulligan, Gil Evans, and John Lewis," thereby setting a jazz precedent in crediting experimental, virtually unknown arrangers. Remember these three movers and shakers; we'll meet them all again soon. In reality, the band was a group of equals, although Miles took charge—and later the credit, much to Gerry Mulligan's disgust. The residency only lasted a week and was heard by a mere handful of people; the band might have folded had not an enthusiast from Capitol Records gotten them into a studio for three sessions in 1949–50 to record 12 tracks.

According to the history books, what was performed in the Royal Roost and then later recorded has become the stuff of legend. For these sessions mark the birth of "cool jazz," which was to dominate jazz throughout the 1950s, win it a huge audience, and make Davis, Mulligan, and many more into major jazz stars.

Leave the history books aside and listen to the music, and you may well wonder what all the fuss is about. Fifty years on, the pieces sound almost commonplace, the mellow brass, reeds, and piano all too smooth for their own good. Emotionally restrained and musically refined, yes, but sophisticated? So what are we talking here—rated or overrated, cool or just dull? I leave it to you to decide. But think on this: cool jazz—it might seem trite now, but you heard it here first. Just because it doesn't shout, doesn't mean it doesn't count.

> **ALL THAT JAZZ**
>
> *The Real Birth of the Cool* (Bandstand): live broadcasts from the Royal Roost Club, New York, September 1948; *The Birth of the Cool* (Capitol): 12 numbers recorded in studio sessions from January and April 1949, and March 1950.
>
> **GERRY MULLIGAN**— *Re-birth of the Cool* (GRP): a 1992 remake of the original sessions with some of the original musicians, unfortunately not including Miles, who had died the previous year.

Miles Davis: no other jazz performer was to go through so many changes— and no one makes more separate appearances in this book!

1953 The Samaritans helpline is founded by Rev. Chad Varah at St. Stephen's Church, Walbrook, London.

1953 A woman is impregnated with frozen sperm at the University of Iowa.

1954 In Obninsk, USSR, nuclear power plants produce energy for the first time.

Pacific Jazz

Publicity for the Haig Club was handled by Richard Bock, who was so enamored by the Mulligan–Baker sound that he began to record the group, setting up Pacific Jazz Records for the purpose in summer 1952. Early hits established the label as the main outlet for West Coast cool musicians, recording saxophonists Art Pepper and Lee Konitz and guitarist Wes Montgomery among others. Album covers reflected its location—all sunny boulevards, sandy shores, and, in the case of *Chet Baker and Crew*, sailboats and short sleeves.

1952~1956

Walking on Eggshells
Gerry Mulligan and Chet Baker

Cool jazz: a deliberate turning away from the spontaneity and excitement of bop toward a more measured music concentrating more on composition than on improvisation. Cool jazz is marked by emotional restraint and subdued performance. So with the definition out of the way, who's cool and who's not, other than the quintessentially cool Miles Davis?

Caught between microphones: Gerry Mulligan, the clean-looking but far from clean-living baritone master of cool.

The epitome of cool is *Chesney "Chet" Baker* (1929–88). With chiseled cheekbones, dark hair, and darker eyes, and a great line in T-shirts and moody photographs, Chet Baker was the James Dean of jazz—youthful, rebellious, and also a junkie, as were so many others in his day. More importantly, he was a fine improviser, playing his trumpet like Miles— understated, lyrical, and direct, with no frills or embellishments. He was

also a good singer, in a crooner sort of way. His partner in crime (and in drugs, for a time) was *Gerry MULLIGAN* (1927–96), one of our trio of famous arrangers from the Birth of the Cool. Mulligan was also goodish looking— tall, thin, with red hair—and played the baritone saxophone. An ungainly instrument, in his hands it danced.

In 1952 Mulligan was playing a regular Monday-night gig at The Haig, a small, converted bungalow on Wilshire Boulevard in Los Angeles that was barely able to seat its audience of 80. The house piano was so poor that Mulligan avoided using it, forming instead a quartet with just Baker's

1955 Walt Disney's Disneyland theme park opens in California.

1955 Kentucky Fried Chicken goes on sale in the U.S.

1956 Elvis Presley's *Heartbreak Hotel* is a massive hit on both sides of the Atlantic.

Cool and casual, a study in style: Chet Baker.

ALL THAT JAZZ

CHET BAKER—*The Best of Chet Baker Plays; Let's Get Lost: The Best of Chet Baker Sings; Chet Baker and Crew* (all Pacific Jazz).

GERRY MULLIGAN—*The Best of the Gerry Mulligan Quartet with Chet Baker* (Pacific Jazz).

LENNIE TRISTANO—*The Complete Lennie Tristano* (Mercury): early sessions from 1946–47; *Lennie Tristano/The New Tristano* (Rhino/ Atlantic): sessions from 1955–61, including Lee Konitz.

trumpet, bass, and drums. No more the monologues of bop improvisers, or the shouting matches of numerous bop workouts, for without a piano to anchor the band in chords, Mulligan and Baker exploited the melodic freedom available by quietly intertwining their solos and supporting lines around each other as if in casual conversation. Tunes were mid-tempo and undemonstrative, and the total effect almost orchestral in the way the deep register of the baritone sax complemented and blended with the higher-register trumpet.

This blend of cool music quickly found its audience, and the quartet's recording of *My Funny Valentine*, complete with famous Baker solo, was an instant hit. But within a year the group broke up when Mulligan, returning from a three-month prison sentence for drug offenses in summer 1953, found Baker seeking to treble his wages on the back of his newfound celebrity status, and refused to pay up. The quartet's recipe for success had been simple, and was to be copied by many: melodic solo lines with beautiful accompaniment, a light, airy sound, accessible tunes, first-rate jazz, and looks to die for.

Cool moves

Cool jazz had two distinct strands— the sensuous, semi-orchestral approach of Miles and Mulligan, and the intellectual rigor of the blind Chicago pianist Lennie Tristano (1919–78). Stripping out all emotion from his music, Tristano was an austere improviser devoid of flashy effects. For many, his work was t oo cerebral, but he encouraged disciples such as Konitz to experiment, even if for many of them that meant striving to sound more like pianists than the saxophonists they all were.

Cooler than cool: Lennie Tristano had an exigent style.

1951 John Paul Getty, the 58-year-old oil baron, is the world's richest man.

1954 In Boston, the first successful kidney transplant takes place, from Richard Herrick to his twin brother, Ronald.

1957 Dr. Seuss's children's book *The Cat in the Hat* becomes a bestseller.

1951~1964

Way Out West

Cool Music on the West Coast

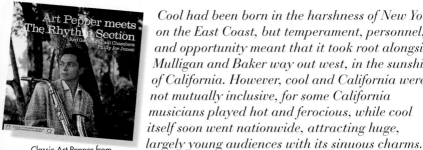

Classic Art Pepper from 1957 with Miles Davis's rhythm section.

Cool had been born in the harshness of New York on the East Coast, but temperament, personnel, and opportunity meant that it took root alongside Mulligan and Baker way out west, in the sunshine of California. However, cool and California were not mutually inclusive, for some California musicians played hot and ferocious, while cool itself soon went nationwide, attracting huge, largely young audiences with its sinuous charms.

Nor was cool synonymous with white musicians, although most West Coast musicians were inevitably white. What it was synonymous with was style, reflecting an upwardly mobile population in the increasingly affluent 1950s, who enjoyed easy listening with a veneer of intellectualism. The leading figures out on the coast— remember, America looks west from New York, not east from Los Angeles—were a mixed bag, but they were united in a wish to move beyond bop to experiment with new sounds.

The sensuous, Milesian side of cool was dominated by Gerry Mulligan, with valve trombonist *Bob Brookmeyer* (b.1929) replacing Baker in the pianoless quartet

The Dave Brubeck Quartet. Brubeck is second from right, Paul Desmond second from left.

Dave Brubeck

White, West Coast, intellectual—pianist Dave Brubeck (b.1920) is surely the very epitome of cool. After all, his quartet wowed every college campus, *Take Five* sold a million copies in 1961, and his alto sax player Paul Desmond (1924–77) was one of the finest cool soloists. Yet for many, Brubeck embodies the term "too clever by half," his heady mix of Bach and modern European composition, complex time signatures, hamfisted chords, and straight-ahead jazz over-egging an already rich concoction. A product of his times, but an enduring one.

1961 Cambridge student revue *Beyond the Fringe* debuts in London's West End.

1963 Frank Sinatra, Jr., is kidnapped from a California hotel room. His father pays $240,000 to have him released.

1964 France and Britain agree to construct a Channel Tunnel.

THE PLAN

before Mulligan left for New York, big bands, and even wider fame. Alto saxophonist *Art PEPPER* (b.1925–82) started out in clean-cut cool style, although drugs and prison turned him into a more emotional player by the end of the 1950s. Other names to watch out for: alto saxophonist *Bud SHANK* (b.1926) and drummer *Shelly MANNE* (1920–84), shop steward of cool who, from 1960, ran the popular Shelly's Manne-Hole club.

The Tristano side of cool was represented by *Shorty ROGERS* (1924–94), a trumpeter-composer whose series of bands experimented with different textures and odd scales. Also experimental was clarinetist *Jimmy GIUFFRE* (b.1921), composer of the original *Four Brothers* theme for Woody Herman and a Rogers sideman, who increasingly took his dark, warm tone and relaxed phrasing in a more individual direction. His great trio with Brookmeyer and guitarist Jim Hall (b.1930) defines cool for most people, playing *The Train and the River* behind the credits of that all-time cool movie, *Jazz on a Summer's Day*, a record of the 1958 Newport Jazz Festival.

COOL AND COZY

In retrospect, it can be seen that cool music was highly incestuous. Mulligan, Pepper, Shank, Manne, and Rogers were all former sidemen in the Stan Kenton Band, and the same small group of musicians—many of them professional studio artists who worked on film soundtracks and

---

ALL THAT JAZZ

DAVE BRUBECK—*Jazz at Oberlin* (OJC): a 1953 college date; *Time Out* and *Greatest Hits* (both Columbia): all the hits with Paul Desmond.

JIMMY GIUFFRE—*The Jimmy Giuffre 3* (Atlantic): a 1956 session including *The Train and the River; Hollywood and Newport, 1957–58* (Fresh Sounds): a live *Train* at Newport.

SHELLY MANNE—*The West Coast Sound* (OJC).

GERRY MULLIGAN—*Pleyel Concerts* (Vogue, two volumes): a live 1954 concert from Paris with Brookmeyer.

ART PEPPER—*Meets the Rhythm Section* (OJC): the section in question on loan from the classic Miles Davis Quintet; *Smack Up* and *Intensity* (both OJC): two classic sessions from 1960.

SHORTY ROGERS—*The Big Shorty Rogers Express* (RCA): 1953–56 sessions with Pepper and Giuffre.

BUD SHANK—*Bud Shank Quartet* (Fresh Sound).

---

recording dates—crop up on each other's records, play at the same few clubs (The Lighthouse at Hermosa Beach, The Haig), and record for the same few labels. But hey, what's wrong with intimacy, when the sun is shining and the music sounds so good?

Jimmy Giuffre, creator of what he called "folk jazz."

1954 The vaccine for polio prevention goes on trial in New York City.

1961 "Golf ball" electric typewriters make their first appearance.

1962 *Telstar* by the Tornados is the first British record to top the American charts.

1952~1974

Chamber Jazz
The Modern Jazz Quartet

The vibraphone.

The MJQ performing in tastefully lit surroundings, as one would expect from a group more at home in the concert hall than some lowdown dive.

Once again we return to the Birth of the Cool sessions, this time to pick up on another of that famous trio of arrangers: John LEWIS (b.1920), a bop pianist whose composing and arranging skills made him much in demand. In 1951 he formed a quartet with vibraphonist Milt JACKSON (b.1923), alongside bassist Ray BROWN (b.1926) and drummer Kenny CLARKE (1914–85). Operating as a collective, the group was known as the Modern Jazz Quartet by the time Percy HEATH (b.1923) replaced Brown in 1952. Three years later, Connie KAY (1927–94) replaced Clarke, and the MJQ was complete, unchanging through an official retirement in 1974 and regular reunions in the 1980s until Kay's death in 1994.

Third Stream

In their use of classical forms and structures, MJQ was in the forefront of Third Stream music, a term coined in 1957 by composer Gunther Schuller at a lecture in Brandeis University, Massachusetts. Schuller (b.1925), French horn player on the *Birth of the Cool* sessions, believed that improvising jazz musicians could learn from score-based musicians and vice versa, forging a Third Stream combining classical music with jazz. Third Stream music was much in vogue in the 1950s, but was heavily criticized for being neither one thing nor the other. Like most lifeforms that live in the middle of the road, it suffered the ultimate penalty, soon run over by heavier musical traffic passing in both directions.

Few groups have lasted so long or been so popular as MJQ, yet the nature of its appeal is difficult to grasp. On one hand MJQ exudes snob appeal—its music is firmly grounded in European classical music, combining elements of the baroque, such as counterpoint and fugue, with considerable melodic variation, complex structures, and a reliance on composition rather than improvisation. This much is due to the classical piano training of John Lewis, who wrote numerous fugues, rondos, and suites for the band, often

1963 In Camden, London, the world's first macrobiotic restaurant opens.

1965 Sixties fashion queen Mary Quant designs the miniskirt.

1974 Patty Hearst is kidnapped by the "Symbionese Liberation Army," which demands that her father, publisher R̲ ̲I̲ ̲ ̲ ̲ ̲ ̲ ̲ ̲ ̲ ̲ ̲ millions to the poor.

ALL THAT JAZZ

The Artistry of the Modern Jazz Quartet (Prestige) and *Django* (OJC): early days from 1952–55; *Concorde* (OJC): a 1955 set with the perfect four; *Dedicated to Connie* (Atlantic, 2 CDs): a 1960 concert issued in honor of Connie Kay after his death; *Lonely Woman* (Atlantic); *MJQ 40* (Atlantic, 4 CDs): 54 of the best from 1952–88.

with 18th-century French titles. On the other hand, MJQ is a jazz band in the best cool style, and in Milt Jackson it has one of the foremost blues and bop improvisers. What results from this meeting of opposites is, in its quiet, reserved way, truly radical, for in abandoning the usual theme and improvised solos of most jazz works in favor of formal compositions with every move planned, MJQ changed the nature of jazz performance.

One man and his bass: the MJQ's original bass player, Ray Brown.

Intellectualism run riot this all may be, but for those who like their jazz cool and calm, the well-crafted quality of an MJQ performance—on disk or on stage—is always to be relied upon. Just because every phrase the group plays has been weighed, measured, and prepared for immaculate presentation, don't ignore the powerful undercurrents of jazz that flow beneath the calm surface. Chamber jazz played in tuxedos, yes, but in the hands of MJQ, what's wrong with the occasional bit of dressing up?

HIP CATS

All four members of MJQ had careers outside the group. **John Lewis** *recorded many sets under his own name and pursued his interest in Third Stream music, setting up the Lennox School of Jazz Summer School with Gunther Schuller in 1959 and, in 1977, becoming professor of music at City College, New York.* **Milt Jackson** *had a flourishing career as sideman on numerous records, working with everyone from Coleman Hawkins to Sonny Rollins.* **Percy Heath** *was the quintessential sideman, playing on one of Ornette Coleman's early, epoch-making albums in 1958 and doing occasional gigs with his younger saxophonist brother Jimmy (b. 1926). But it was* **Connie Kay** *who had the most remarkable career, playing on many R&B studio sessions—notably Joe Turner's* Shake, Rattle, and Roll—*as well as Van Morrison's seminal 1968 rock album* Astral Weeks.

1956 The first Eurovision song contest is held in Lugano, Switzerland.

1957 The Teddy Boy craze is responsible for the first real "youth tribe."

1958 *Billboard* magazine launches the Hot 100 singles chart.

1956~1964
The Great American Songbook
Ella Fitzgerald

Ella Fitzgerald: the hairstyle may look dated, but the voice will ring true forever.

A life of lucky breaks, although Ella FITZGERALD (1917–96) would be the first to point out she had worked hard to achieve them. Her first break came in 1934 when she won a talent contest at that notoriously critical venue, the Apollo Theatre in Harlem, and was promptly hired by Chick Webb to sing in his big band. She became a celebrity of the Savoy Ballroom—the main New York swing venue—and had a huge hit in 1938 with the lightweight A-tisket, a-tasket.

Her second break came in 1939 when Webb died and Ella, barely 22, took the band over and ran it until it folded in 1942. The third was her association with the Jazz at the Philharmonic tours after 1946, which made her solo career, but it was her fourth, in 1956, that elevated Ella into a class of her own.

J ATP impresario Norman Granz felt Ella was not being promoted properly by her record company, Decca, and in 1956 poached her to join his newly founded Verve label. Rather than release a random collection of songs, Granz hit upon the idea of a concept album—a songbook dedicated to a single American songwriter. Cole Porter got the treatment first, and so successful was the result that Ella set to work singing her way through the Great American Songbook. The best, the most

1959 Earth receives its first pictures of the dark side of the moon, transmitted by the Soviet spacecraft *Luna III*.

1960 Frank Sinatra, Dean Martin, and Sammy Davis, Jr., open the Democratic Party Convention by singing the national anthem.

1961 Jaguar launches its classic E-Type sports coupé.

Betty Carter, nicknamed Betty Bebop by Lionel Hampton: a jazz chanteuse with a modern touch.

famous, and some lesser known works of Harold Arlen, the Gershwins, Rodgers and Hart, Jerome Kern, Irving Berlin, and Duke Ellington were dusted off and polished up by an Ella at the height of her considerable powers, supported by an orchestra led by such famous arrangers as Nelson Riddle or Billy May. To attempt a song cycle of this length was unprecedented in popular music, and it established her reputation as the First Lady of jazz.

Sarah Vaughan, who, like Ella, won an amateur contest at Harlem's Apollo Theater and never looked back, her career lasting almost 50 years.

ELLA'S ACHIEVEMENT

Ella was never a diva like Sarah Vaughan, nor did she have the aura of a Billie Holiday, but what she did possess was one of the most complete and assured techniques of any jazz singer. Driving swing, fine pitch, perfect timing, and instrumentlike improvisatory skills were married to an optimistic, innocent view of the world that gave her songs a radiant quality. She made it all sound so easy—she could have sung the telephone book and made it swing—but that ease hid considerable skill. It also hid a personal toughness, for Ella was the indestructible musician, on the road for up to 45 weeks a year and performing well into her seventies. The last word goes to Ira Gershwin: "I never knew how good our songs were until I heard Ella Fitzgerald sing them." What finer tribute could there be?

Women singers

Unfairly, the most famous women in jazz are all singers. Of these, Ella Fitzgerald is renowned, but she had her rivals. Sarah Vaughan (1924–90) had perfect intonation and real improvisatory skills, but her effortless mastery could sometimes become self-parody. Dinah Washington (1924–63) suffered in different ways, for her skills at rhythm and blues, pop, gospel, jazz, and ballads meant many overlooked just how good she was, whatever she sang. Her showstopping performance at the 1958 Newport Jazz Festival, captured on *Jazz on a Summer's Day*, set the record straight. Carmen McRae (1922–94) was a late starter, recording nothing under her own name until 1954, but making up for it with fine records featuring her bop-influenced style and smoky delivery. Newer on the block was Betty Carter (1929–98), whose stage performances were legendary for the relationship she established with her audience and her feminist slant on a song.

1953 Englishman Edmund Hillary and Sherpa Tenzing Norgay become the first men to reach the summit of Everest.

1953 Armistice signed to end the three-year war between Communist North Korea and American-backed South Korea.

1954 Coffee culture invades Britain as coffee bars open across the country.

1953~1956
Hard Bop
Clifford Brown and Miles Davis

The muted trumpet.

Labels again, I'm sorry to say, and this time the label is far from clear. Look at it this way—in reaction to bop came cool, and in quick reaction to cool came bop again. Not that bop ever went away, you understand. But to distinguish the 1950s version from the 1940s original, critics have termed it hard bop. The musicians involved made no such distinction, any more than they restricted themselves to playing hard bop, or the soul jazz (or modal jazz or free jazz) about to hit you in a few pages' time. But labels act as helpful signposts in showing which way jazz was moving at the time, and who was on which side of the road, for jazz traffic in the 1950s was heavy.

The LP

The introduction in 1948 of the 12" vinyl LP, playing at 33⅓ rpm, transformed jazz during the 1950s. Until then, musicians were restricted to recording only what could fit on a 10" or 12" shellac record played at 78 rpm—a maximum of 4 minutes per side. By contrast, musicians could play live for as long as stamina, audience, and the management allowed. The LP, with its playing time of about 25 minutes per side, led to increasing convergence between recorded and live jazz. Longer does not always mean better, however, as some garrulous endeavors testify.

Hard bop was an earthy, extrovert music, with loudish drumming, light piano lines, superb bass playing, soulful tunes, and a good dash of the blues. It was an urban music—its main practitioners came from Detroit and Philadelphia—and Blue Note recorded most of it. Lots of young, mainly black, musicians played hard bop, but two trumpeters stand out.

In 1954 Charlie Parker's drummer, Max Roach, set up a quintet with trumpeter *Clifford BROWN* (1930–56), a Gillespie

Max Roach, a powerhouse drummer for more than 50 years, from be-bop in the 1940s to experiments with free jazz and elements from rap and hip-hop.

1955 Grace Kelly and Cary Grant star in Alfred Hitchcock's thriller *To Catch a Thief*, set on the French Riviera.

1956 A workers' uprising in Hungary led by Prime Minister Imre Nagy is suppressed by Soviet tanks.

1956 Soviet First Secretary Nikita Khrushchev denounces the crimes of the Stalin era.

Mute it

The sound of the trumpet was revolutionized in 1954 when Miles Davis became the first jazz musician to use a stemless metal harmon mute. The mute fits into the bell of the trumpet, and the air is forced through it, muffling the sound. Miles played with the mute close up to the microphone, emitting a remote, brooding, utterly distinct sound that characterized his playing from then on.

disciple. Brownie, as he was universally known, was a star. Unlike Gillespie, who sometimes sacrificed tone for speed, he sacrificed nothing. Possessed of one of the most perfect trumpet tones in jazz, he exuded warmth in every note he played. Tragedy struck in June 1956 when, along with the band's pianist *Richie POWELL* (1931–56),

One of the most talented of trumpeters, with a burnished tone and a singing delivery, Clifford Brown has influenced every trumpeter to this day.

Brown was killed in a car accident. Roach eventually set up another quintet, this time with trumpeter *Booker LITTLE* (1938–61)—another jazz casualty, this time of uremia at 23—and though he was good, he remained in Brownie's shadow.

After his dalliance with cool and a major run-in with drugs, *Miles DAVIS* (1926–91) played with some of hard bop's finest in the early 1950s until, in 1955, he set up a quintet with tenor saxophonist *John COLTRANE* (1926–67). They were as different as night and day, a restrained Miles in contrast to the hard-driving Coltrane, over a rhythm section, *the* rhythm section to die for: *Red GARLAND* (1923–84) on piano, *Paul CHAMBERS* (1935–69) on bass, and *Philly Joe JONES* (1923–85) on drums. Collectively the quintet was *the* jazz band of the late

1950s; individually it established Miles and then Coltrane as the dominant figures of modern jazz.

Many other musicians played in the hard bop style, such as Sonny Rollins and Charles Mingus, both of whom we come to shortly. But the man who most sums up hard bop was a drummer through whose band everybody who was anybody in jazz for 30 years has passed: Art Blakey.

> ### ALL THAT JAZZ
>
> **MAX ROACH**—*Brownie Lives!* (Fresh Sounds): the quintet live; *Deeds Not Words* (OJC), with Booker Little; *Alone Together* (Verve): the best of Roach.
> **CLIFFORD BROWN**—*Clifford Brown Memorial Album* (Blue Note, 2 CDs).
> **MILES DAVIS**—*Miles Davis* (Blue Note, 2 volumes): Miles finds his feet; *Cookin', Relaxin', Workin', Steamin'* (all Prestige): the classic quintet in 1956; *Chronicle: The Complete Prestige Recordings 1951–1956* (Prestige, 8 CDs).
> **BOOKER LITTLE**—*Out Front* (Candid).

1957 Althea Gibson wins the women's singles at Wimbledon. She is the first black American to be invited to play.

1965 In Britain, cigarette advertising is banned from commercial television.

1980 Compact disk players are launched.

1954~1990

Jazz Is the Message

Art Blakey

Forever on the road with Art Blakey—the Messengers were constantly in flux.

Some groups, such as MJQ, profit from unchanging personnel. Others profit from constant change and renewal. Of these, the Jazz Messengers is the prime example, run for 35 years by drummer Art BLAKEY (1919–90), yet never keeping the same personnel for more than a couple of years. Through its ranks passed every hard bop player worth raising a glass to, serving as the finishing school for musicians who, when fully fledged, left the Messengers' nest and took wing to greater fame and glory.

Blakey emerged out of the Fletcher Henderson Orchestra in 1943–44 into bop. In 1947 he organized a rehearsal band known as the Seventeen Messengers and recorded with an octet known simply as the Jazz Messengers. Then he went to Africa for a year to learn about Islamic culture—he later converted to Islam and was known as Abdullah ibn Buhaina—and returned to work with Parker, Monk, and others. By now a fine drummer with incendiary power, propulsive swing, and a fine line in whipcrack snare-drum rolls and a persistent cymbal beat, he set up a quintet early in 1954 with pianist *Horace SILVER* (b.1928) and trumpeter Clifford Brown, and was recorded live at New York's Birdland. This was the prototype Messengers, and in November 1954, with *Kenny DORHAM* (1924–72) on trumpet and *Hank MOBLEY* (1930–86) on tenor sax, the group entered the studio to record an album under Horace Silver's name. The following year the group became a cooperative, and when Silver left in 1956, Blakey took over.

ALL THAT JAZZ

ART BLAKEY—*A Night at Birdland* (Blue Note, 2 volumes): the prototype Messengers with Clifford Brown in a 1954 live set.
HORACE SILVER—*Horace Silver and the Jazz Messengers* (Blue Note): a 1954 studio session with the first edition of Dorham and Mobley.
THE JAZZ MESSENGERS—*At the Café Bohemia* (Blue Note, 2 volumes): the first edition live in 1955; *Moanin'* (Blue Note), with Morgan, Golson, and Timmons in 1958; *Mosaic* (Blue Note), with Hubbard and Shorter in 1961; *Keystone 3* (Concord), with the Marsalis brothers in 1982.

1985 Live Aid, a 17-hour rock concert, is broadcast on television and radio to 152 countries, raising $70 million for starving people in Africa.

1986 The United States establishes an official holiday in honor of Martin Luther King, Jr.

1989 President Bush announces his dislike of broccoli. The California Broccoli Shippers Association responds by sending him boxes of the stuff along with some gourmet recipes.

H I P   C A T S

The roll-call of Messengers includes most of the greats of hard bop, with just one member (guess who) a constant for 35 years.

SAXOPHONISTS

Hank Mobley—*1954–56, 1959*; **Jackie McLean**—*1956–58*; **Benny Golson**—*1958–59*; **Wayne Shorter**—*1959–63*; **John Gilmore**—*1964–65*; **Bobby Watson**—*1977–81*; **Branford Marsalis**—*1981–82*; **Donald Harrison**—*1982–84*

TRUMPETERS

Kenny Dorham—*1954–56*, **Donald Byrd**—*1956*; **Lee Morgan**—*1958–61, 1964–65*; **Freddie Hubbard**—*1961–64*; **Woody Shaw**—*1971–72*; **Wynton Marsalis**—*1980–82*; **Terence Blanchard**—*1982–86*

PIANISTS

Horace Silver—*1954–56*; **Bobby Timmons**—*1958–59*; **Cedar Walton**—*1961–64*; **Keith Jarrett**—*1965–66*; **JoAnne Brackeen**—*1969–72*; **Mulgrew Miller**—*1983–86*

DRUMMER

Art Blakey—*1954–90*

Although the group changed constantly in both personnel and extent, it remained true to its hard bop roots, propelled from the drum stool with ferocious drive and a fine line in bluesy melodies. Standout Messengers editions include the 1958 lineup with trumpeter *Lee MORGAN*

(1938–72), saxophonist *Benny GOLSON* (b.1929), who wrote *Blues March*, and pianist *Bobby TIMMONS* (1935–74), who wrote *Moanin'*; the early '60s version with *Wayne SHORTER* (b.1933) on saxophone; and a renascent Messengers with the Marsalis brothers on board in 1981–82. Although jazz changed hugely throughout this period, the Messengers never went out of fashion, a constant powerhouse as indefatigable as its ever-youthful leader.

Art Blakey, the dynamic, percussive driving force behind the Messengers for over 30 years, still going strong toward the end of his career.

1958 In Paris, Yves Saint Laurent holds his first fashion show.

1968 The supersonic speed of Mach 2 is accomplished. The plane, a Tupolev Tu-144, travels at an approximate speed of 1,200 m.p.h.

1972 The New Seekers have a number-one hit in Britain with *I'd Like To Teach The World to Sing.*

1956~present

Saxophone Colossus
Sonny Rollins

Tenor saxophone, Rollins's forte.

Sonny ROLLINS (b.1930) is one of jazz's great enigmas. A saxophone virtuoso with a muscular tone and huge melodic invention, Rollins has never made quite the most of his huge talents. Three times he has retired to rethink his music, yet each time what resulted was slightly less than what went before. Yet on a good night, of which there are still plenty, Rollins imperiously carries all before him, his solo performances in particular marvels of invention, ingenuity, and rip-roaring fun.

Rollins was a product of the bop revolution, but his early efforts were tentative and unformed. So he woodshedded away from New York in 1955, returning to play with the famous Clifford

Rollins in full flight, tenor sax well to the fore.

Brown–Max Roach quintet. He was a saxophonist transformed and, in 1956, recorded what was to become one of hard bop's greatest albums: *Saxophone Colossus*. Each track stands out, but *St. Thomas*, a calypso he was to record again and again, is especially gorgeous.

At this point, Rollins was the top saxophonist in jazz, and great music poured out of him over the next two years. But in 1959 he retired again, this time to ponder the challenge to his supremacy by *John COLTRANE (1926–67)* and the new style of free jazz (don't worry—all will

> ## The Bridge
>
> The Rollins comeback album in 1962 was called *The Bridge*, celebrating his habit when in retirement of practicing on the catwalk of the Williamsburg Bridge in New York City.

1985 Rupert Murdoch, media tycoon from "down under," becomes an American citizen for business reasons.

1993 Queen Elizabeth II becomes the first monarch in Britain to pay income tax.

1996 Gene Kelly, star of *Singin' in the Rain* (1952) and *An American in Paris* (1951), dies in Beverly Hills.

Rollins with the late English saxophonist Ronnie Scott, host to jazz's finest performers.

ALL THAT JAZZ

Saxophone Colossus (OJC): the 1956 set that established Rollins in the first league; *Way Out West* (OJC), *Newk's Time* (Blue Note), *A Night at the Village Vanguard* (Blue Note, 2 volumes): powering through 1957; *The Sound of Sonny/Freedom Suite* (Riverside): two classics from 1957–58; *The Bridge* (Bluebird); *On the Outside* (RCA Bluebird): Rollins meets the new wave in 1962–63; *G Man* (Milestone): live in the 1980s.

embraced fusion music (again, we'll come to this soon) and then slowly reverted to the bop of his youth.

The problem with Rollins is that with so much to choose from, his work is quite inconsistent. High points are matched by dreary lows, with good bands failing to lift him and poor bands perversely prompting him to extravagant displays of virtuosity. Sometimes he plays a song straight, at others he pulls it apart and reconstructs it from the bottom up, adding in snippets of melody drawn from numerous, often unrelated songs (although snatches of every song with "goodnight" in the title have been known to make an appearance), making new music out of the old. For sheer exuberance and *joie de vivre*, Sonny Rollins is (nearly always) unbeatable.

Woodshedding

... as in retiring from the music scene to the proverbial woodshed to practice or experiment with new music. Rollins did it twice, in 1955 and again in 1959–61, as well as abandoning music altogether in 1969–71.

be explained soon). When he returned, playing with free-jazz trumpeter *Don Cherry* (1936–95), little had changed in his style, and, strangely enough, he barely bothered to engage with the new approach. Yet he sounded troubled and at times angry, and as the decade wore on, Rollins's records suggested he was aimless and bored with himself, as if his talent were not being stretched enough. Time for another break, this one to India for spiritual renewal and two years with no music at all. Back again in 1972, he

Classic Rollins, recorded at the Village Vanguard, New York, in 1957.

1958 In London, Samuel Beckett's play *Endgame* is banned for alleged blasphemy.

1960 Alfred Hitchcock's thriller *Psycho* is the most talked-about film of the year.

1961 Bob Dylan plays his first gig at Gerde's Folk City, Greenwich Village, New York.

1955~1966

Mercy, Mercy, Mercy

Soul Jazz

Jimmy Smith took gospel, and the sound of the Hammond organ, into jazz.

Another label, this one a subdivision of hard bop (which is itself a subdivision of bop, which is itself ...). Not really a full-blown style, more a trend in the mid-1950s toward a more soulful, funky style of hard bop with a goodly element of gospel music thrown in for elevating measure. Easier, less frenetic tunes with catchy, repeated hooks are set against a rousing beat, while one instrument dominates proceedings: the extraordinary Hammond organ. But a word of caution—while "funky" is the best word to describe soul jazz, neither funk nor soul has the meaning the two words will acquire in the following decade. We're not talking Aretha Franklin or James Brown here.

A word or two about the Hammond B3 electronic organ. First manufactured in 1935, the Hammond was a vast, ungainly beast just about light enough to be taken on tour. *Jimmy SMITH* (b.1925) was one of the first to grasp its potential, playing walking bass lines on the pedals with his feet, full-blooded chords with his left hand, and fast bop lines with his right. Most importantly, he introduced ideas from gospel music, for the Hammond was the instrument of choice in the black churches. But the gospel feel of soul jazz was less a result of religious belief than of racial pride, for gospel was a homegrown black music of considerable emotional force.

Soul jazz was not the prerogative of the Hammond. Listen for

Trumpet fireworks from Blue Note star Lee Morgan.

1963 In Britain the Great Train Robbery takes place. The raid takes 20 minutes, and the gang gets away with £2.5 million.

1964 In Switzerland, long-life milk is developed by Verbands Mölkerei.

1966 Skinny 17-year-old Twiggy, the original "waif," becomes the most famous fashion model in the world.

ALL THAT JAZZ

CANNONBALL ADDERLEY—*Somethin' Else* (Blue Note): 1958 meeting with Miles Davis; *Mercy, Mercy, Mercy* (Capitol).
RAY CHARLES—*Soul Brothers/Soul Meeting, Ray Charles at Newport* (both Atlantic).
HERBIE HANCOCK—*Takin' Off*; **LEE MORGAN**—*The Sidewinder*;
HORACE SILVER—*Song for My Father*
JIMMY SMITH—*The Sermon* (all Blue Note).

Ray Charles, a man to defeat all attempts at labeling.

the bluesy alto saxophone of *Julian "Cannonball" ADDERLEY* (1928–75)—his nickname meaning cannibal, because he ate everything as a kid—and the bright trumpet of *Lee MORGAN* (1938–72), who provided a massive hit for Blue Note with *The Sidewinder*. Pianist *Bobby TIMMONS* (1935–74) provided the Jazz Messengers with one of the group's enduring party pieces—*Moanin'*—while *Horace SILVER* (b.1928) penned a stream of soul jazz standards, notably *Song for My Father*, as did newcomer *Herbie HANCOCK* (b.1940) in the 1960s with tracks like *Canteloupe Island*. But as the 1960s wore on, many pianists took up the electric piano, with which *Ray CHARLES* (b.1930) had already experimented. And so we're into fusion...

Ray Charles

When is a jazz musician not a jazz musician? A stupid question, but one answer is, when he also plays soul, gospel, blues, C&W, and R&B, and is called Ray Charles. Another blind pianist (remember Tatum and Tristano, and we haven't even mentioned George Shearing), Charles began as a Nat King Cole acolyte, but was firmly into gospel and R&B by the mid-1950s. As a vocalist and big-band leader, his mantra of *Genius + Soul = Jazz* (a 1960 bestselling album) turns each concert into a Holy-Roller fusion of numerous styles, from the romantic yearning of *Georgia on My Mind* to the uproarious *What'd I Say*. Charles's importance is as the guiding force of the transformation of black popular music from R&B to soul. Not really jazz, or not just jazz, but it would be stupid to consider the history of jazz without him.

1956 Nikita Khrushchev tells Western ambassadors, "History is on our side. We will bury you."

1957 Audiences around the world are shocked by the opening sequence of Roger Vadim's film *And God Created Woman*, in which Brigitte Bardot appears nude.

1959 The Xerox 914, the first photocopier able to produce copies at the press of a button, is launched by Haloid.

1956~1966

Oh Yeah!

Charles Mingus

The combative, temperamental, larger-than-life Charles MINGUS (1922–79) was one of jazz's iconoclasts. A double-bass player, pianist, composer, arranger, and band leader, Mingus inspired and infuriated in equal measure. His large-scale compositions rivaled anything by Ellington, and he transformed 1920s New Orleans-style collective improvisation into an essential part of modern jazz. Yet listen to any Mingus piece before 1956, and you wonder if you've got the right man.

Who's afraid of a score? Not Charles Mingus. Unlike some jazz musicians, he was as accomplished at large-scale composition as he was at improvisation.

Mingus began playing bass in the 1940s with the big bands of Louis Armstrong and Lionel Hampton. By the late 1940s he was into bop, playing with Charlie Parker, and in the early 1950s evolved into the epitome of cool. Had he recorded nothing else after 1955, he would have been considered a good but uninspiring technician. But Mingus was also a thinker, adept at analyzing his own music. Accordingly, he

ALL THAT JAZZ

Pithecanthropus Erectus, The Clown, Blues and Roots (Atlantic); *Mingus Ah Um* (Columbia), the 1959 masterpiece; *Mingus at Antibes* (Atlantic): live and roaring in 1960; *The Black Saint and the Sinner Lady* and *Mingus Mingus Mingus Mingus* (both MCA): the height of his powers in 1963; *Thirteen Pictures* (Rhino, 3 CDs): an anthology of the best from 1952–77.

and others set up the Jazz Composers' Workshop in 1953 to perform experimental music. Mingus contributed written arrangements in which improvisation was reduced to a minimum, but he found musical notation restrictive, so in 1955 he set up his own Jazz Workshop, in which he transmitted his ideas by dictating lines to each player. This gave him the freedom he was looking for, and in 1956 he turned his back on his

1960 In Britain, shoe manufacturer R. Griggs and Co. launches German-designed Doctor Marten's workboots.

1963 In the U.S., 12-year-old singer Stevie Wonder releases his first album, *Little Stevie Wonder.*

1966 *Star Trek* launches into television hyperspace.

Politics in jazz

For a long time there wasn't any. Jazz was music for entertainment, although blues singers recorded the oppression endured by blacks. But when jazz became big business, black bands often earned half the takings of white bands, and in integrated bands black musicians suffered the indignity of playing as equals with white men while being forced, in many Southern states, to enter hotels through the back door. Anger at such injustices was channeled through the Civil Rights movement of the 1950s, which involved many musicians. Mingus was incensed by the attempts of Arkansas governor Orval E. Faubus to prevent racial integration in Little Rock, and named *Fables of Faubus* in his derisive honor. These and other sentiments were essentially liberal; the confrontational politics of Black Power were yet to come.

former analytical approach and embraced a music as free-thinking as the man himself.

Pithecanthropus Erectus, a stormy musical description of early humans; *Blues and Roots*, with its uplifting *Wednesday Night Prayer Meeting*; *Mingus Ah Um*, containing *Goodbye Pork Pie Hat*, an affecting tribute to Lester Young: these and more turned jazz performance inside out as he encouraged his musicians to see their solos not as personal expressions but as intrinsic parts of an often hedonistic whole. *The Black Saint and the Sinner Lady* rewrote Ellington and looked forward to some of the massive suites we will visit later, while Mingus struggled to cap everything with the vast *Epitaph*, performed in its entirety only after his death.

After 1963, everything went sour. He failed to find a publisher for his

One of Mingus's best albums, from 1963: layered textures and tonal acrobatics.

autobiography, *Beneath the Underdog,* and his own record company folded. Other attempts to free himself from economic dependence on the white-dominated jazz world also failed, and he retired from public performance in 1966. He returned the following decade, but his fire was exhausted, and he died of multiple sclerosis in 1979. But between 1956 and 1963 he wrote little that was not a masterpiece, and his recorded performances are among the most exhilarating in jazz. Adams's Rules of Jazz concerning misuse of the word "genius" do not apply here.

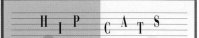

H I P   C A T S

Many famous musicians played with Mingus, but the hard core of Workshop devotees included trombonist **Jimmy Knepper** *(b.1927), saxophonists* **Booker Ervin** *(1930–70) and* **John Handy** *(b.1933), trumpeter* **Ted Curson** *(b.1935), multi-reedsmen* **Roland Kirk** *(1936–77) and* **Eric Dolphy** *(1928–64), of whom more later, pianist* **Jaki Byard** *(b.1922), and drummer* **Dannie Richmond** *(1935–88).*

1958 At a Carnegie Hall benefit concert Danny Kaye conducts the Philharmonic Orchestra—with his feet!

1959 Billy Wilder's successful gangster/jazz musical comedy movie *Some Like It Hot* is released, starring Marilyn Monroe, Tony Curtis, and Jack Lemmon.

1960 The supersonic bomb, Convair B-58, is designed.

1957~1962
Sketches of Gil
Gil Evans

The flugelhorn

The flugelhorn is a trumpet-shaped instrument related to the bugle. It made its first appearance in jazz in 1936, played in Woody Herman's band by Joe Bishop (1907–76), but was rarely heard again until the 1950s, when Shorty Rogers took it up. Miles played it on *Miles Ahead, Porgy and Bess*, and the *Concierto* from *Sketches of Spain*, although it is often hard to tell flugelhorn from trumpet, such was Miles's mastery of both instruments. Still a rarity in jazz, the flugelhorn is useful in that it has a mellow, more hornlike sound than the brassier trumpet.

We have a slight difference of opinion here. On one hand, three of the best-loved albums in jazz appear under the name of Miles Davis and feature him in beautiful, enigmatic form. On the other, it is not Miles in charge, nor is his usual (and extraordinary) quintet playing with him. So who do we praise for Miles Ahead, Porgy and Bess, *and* Sketches of Spain—*Miles the soloist, or Gil Evans the arranger?*

Gil Evans, a magician of sound who could produce a unique richness of tone and texture.

I t was an unlikely pairing to begin with—quiet, Canadian arranger *Gil Evans* (1912–88) and volatile, hard-spoken American trumpeter *Miles Davis* (1926–91). We've met them both before, at *The Birth of the Cool* sessions, where Gil Evans was the third of those famous arrangers—remember? Musically they sparked, but at the time their collaboration was brief.

Astute promotion soon reunited them. After his surprise success at the 1955 Newport Jazz Festival—most people felt

he was too strung out on drugs ever to play properly again—Miles was signed by Columbia. To distance their new signing from the quintet albums flooding out of Prestige, his old record company, Columbia suggested a new approach: Miles the innovative trumpeter fronting a state-of-the-art arranger's band. Miles jumped at the offer and chose Gil as his arranger. Gil readily agreed and listed 16 instruments to create the sound he wanted. Surprisingly, Columbia agreed to bankroll the pair.

Gil's arrangements were sublime. Velvet-soft trumpets, gliding trombones, deep French horns, and a deeper tuba provided a sumptuous cushion of sound, with flutes and clarinets adding lightness on top. The

1961 Austrian Arnold Schoenberg becomes the first musician to use a computer to create a piece of music.

1962 Anthony Burgess's controversial novel A Clockwork Orange is published.

1962 Cans that have tabs to open them are introduced by the Iron City Beer Company, Pittsburgh.

Gil after Miles

Away from Miles, Gil Evans issued a number of albums under his own name, all featuring his seemingly ad hoc, made-on-the-premises arrangements which threaten to fall apart but never do. He didn't have a regular band, but his reputation was such that the great and the good lined up to work with him. As Evans aged, he got younger, and by the late 1960s, prompted by Miles, was expressing admiration for the music of rock guitarist Jimi Hendrix. A collaboration between Hendrix and Davis in 1970 came to nothing when Davis demanded too much money, so Hendrix turned to Gil. Unfortunately, Hendrix died before the project came to fruition, but Evans carried on with the arrangements, which were released in 1974. Hendrix songs remained in the Evans repertoire to the end, notably with the superb Monday night orchestra he led weekly at Sweet Basil's Club in New York throughout the 1980s.

big surprise was Miles, as featured soloist, mainly playing the flugelhorn. Between May 1957 and March 1960 three classic albums were recorded: *Miles Ahead*, ten arrangements of new pieces mixed with such oddities as *The Maids of Cadiz*, by 19th-century French composer Léo Delibes; *Porgy and Bess*, featuring

arrangements of 12 songs from George Gershwin's musical; and *Sketches of Spain*, much of which was taken up by a 16-minute arrangement of the adagio from Joaquín Rodrigo's *Concierto de Aranjuez*, Miles soloing in place of the original Spanish guitar. Other tracks on *Sketches of Spain* included a 1915 ballet score by Manuel de Falla, a recreation of a Good Friday religious ceremony, and a quasi-flamenco blues piece. It wasn't as if Miles or Gil had ever visited Spain!

Was this jazz or classical music—Third Stream gone mad—and was it Miles or Gil? Critics and fans alike ignored the niceties and bought all three albums by the truckload. Although the two collaborated on other projects right up to Gil's death in 1988, nothing matched the sublime majesty achieved by Miles and Gil on these three peerless recordings.

ALL THAT JAZZ

MILES DAVIS—*Miles Ahead; Porgy and Bess; Sketches of Spain; Miles Davis at Carnegie Hall 1961* (2 CDs)—with a live *Concierto; Miles Davis/Gil Evans: the Complete Columbia Studio Recordings* (6 CDs)—the three classics plus other material up to 1968 (all Columbia). **GIL EVANS**—*Out of the Cool* (MCA); *Into the Hot* (Impulse!); *Plays the Music of Jimi Hendrix* (Bluebird).

Miles and Gil at work: an empathetic relationship that produced three classics.

1959 The first Barbie doll is launched by Mattel and costs $3.

1959 The Messerschmitt KR200, or "Bubble car," hits the streets of London and the Morris Mini-Minor goes on sale in Britain.

1959 The word "psychedelic" is introduced into the English language.

PSYCHEDELIC

1957~1960
Kind of Blue
Miles Davis

Another label now, but whatever I say at this point is sort of irrelevant, for the best example of modal jazz is Kind of Blue, *recorded by Miles Davis in 1959 and generally recognized to be the most important jazz record ever released. More words have been written about this one album than any other in jazz. Modal or not, what counts here is the luminous beauty of this music, so I'll tread carefully around the technical minefield that is modal jazz.*

Kind of Blue, and kind of essential for every record collection.

The first point to make clear is that Miles did not invent modal jazz—for the ideas had been around among jazz technicians for some time, notably pianist Bill Evans—but he was the first to popularize it. He experimented with this new way of improvising on the soundtrack of the film *Ascenseur pour l'échafaud*—a Louis Malle thriller starring Jeanne Moreau—which he recorded with four Paris-based musicians, including MJQ founder drummer Kenny Clarke, in Paris one night in December 1957. All the music—a series of ten snippets to accompany various scenes—was totally improvised, and turned a mediocre film into a great soundtrack. Back in America, he firmed up his approach on the title track of *Milestones* (credited as *Miles* in the album-cover notes), a 40-bar structure involving two related modal scales on which the musicians improvise.

By 1959 Miles had the rudiments of modal jazz in place, and in March and April he recorded the five tracks of *Kind of Blue*, at least two of them modal: *So What* and *Flamenco Sketches*. All the pieces are

> **" ☆ "**
>
> ### *Kind of mix-up*
>
> On the original cover notes for *Kind of Blue*, pianist Bill Evans's notes muddled up the order of *Flamenco Sketches* and *All Blues*. Endless critical confusion has flowed ever since, but it's obvious which is which when you listen to the music.

> **ALL THAT JAZZ**
>
> **BILL EVANS**—*Everybody Digs Bill Evans* (OJC)—a 1958 recording featuring *Peace Piece*, the modal prototype for *Flamenco Sketches*.
> **MILES DAVIS**—*Ascenseur pour l'échafaud* (Fontana); *Milestones* (Columbia)—the 1958 warm-up; *Kind of Blue* (Columbia)—the masterpiece.
> **JOHN COLTRANE**—*My Favorite Things* (Atlantic).

1959 Two monkeys, Able and Baker, are sent into space by NASA and return safely.

1959 U.S. authorities ban D.H. Lawrence's raunchy novel *Lady Chatterley's Lover*.

1959 The Guggenheim Museum, designed by Frank Lloyd Wright, opens in New York. The designer dies 6 months before its completion.

slow and spare, and the musicians were handed outlines of the music only on the mornings of recording. Other than *Flamenco Sketches*, everything was recorded in just one take, giving the album a spontaneity and immediacy that sings out in every note.

Modal jazz

Modal jazz is difficult to define but easy to recognize. Basically, modes are scales using different combinations of the eight notes available. So modal jazz is a style in which musicians improvise using only the notes of a modal scale, or chords using only those notes, rather than the many notes drawn from a frequently changing progression of chords, as in bop. Although both major and minor scales are technically modes, what we're talking here are such exotics as aeolian, dorian, lydian, and phrygian, where the sequence of intervals between notes of the scale produces sounds more familiar in medieval church or Indian or Spanish music than jazz. Because there are no chord changes, modal jazz often creates unhurried, meditative, sometimes melancholic music, although both Coltrane and Miles (in his jazz-funk phase) upped the modal ante considerably.

Miles continued to develop modal jazz, as did John Coltrane, most famously on a version of *My Favorite Things*, as sung by Julie Andrews in *The Sound of Music*. What counts, though, is not individual tracks but the modal method itself. With modes, Miles introduced to jazz a more flexible method of melodic improvisation using a single scale or mode for long stretches rather than selecting notes from each consecutive chord. That might sound like swapping one restriction for another, but in reality it freed musicians up.

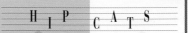

HIP CATS

The sextets that recorded Milestones *and* Kind of Blue *were stellar in membership. Both albums used two saxophonists:* **Julian "Cannonball" Adderley** (1928–75) *was a soul-jazz alto player whose cheerful, relaxed lines contrasted with the serious austerity of tenor saxophonist* **John Coltrane** (1926–67: *more about him later). The* Milestones *rhythm section was the one that recorded those classic Davis quintet albums for Prestige in 1956: pianist* **Red Garland** (1923–84), *bass player* **Paul Chambers** (1935–69), *and drummer* **Philly Joe Jones** (1923–85). *On* Kind of Blue *the main pianist was* **Bill Evans** (1929–80), *whose allusive, impressionistic lines created the right mood of sparseness.* **Wynton Kelly** (1931–71) *played a sparkly solo on one track.* Chambers *remained on bass;* **Jimmy Cobb** (b.1929) *played drums.*

Miles with style: muted trumpet, loud carpet.

1959 The hovercraft, designed by Christopher Cockerell, makes its first journey across the English Channel.

1960 Twenty-year-old Chubby Checker has a hit with *Let's Twist Again*, bringing with it the Twist dance craze.

1961 Satirical British magazine *Private Eye* is launched.

1958~1965

The Shape of Jazz to Come

Ornette Coleman

The start of the Coleman free-form revolution.

*"I don't know what he's playing, but it's not jazz,"
observed Dizzy Gillespie. "The only really new
thing since the mid-40s innovations of Gillespie,
Parker, and Monk," according to John Lewis of
the MJQ. Take your pick. If you have listened to
every record so far listed in this book, very little
would have shocked you—all approachable stuff.
But at this point the parting of the ways occurs,
for what you are about to receive will not sound
like jazz as you know it. But persevere, for in this
harsh, free world, a raw beauty exists.*

As Miles was developing modal jazz on the East Coast, *Ornette COLEMAN* (b.1930) was inventing free jazz in Los Angeles. Coleman was a self-taught alto saxophonist with a background in R&B who, bluntly, heard and played things differently from everyone else. Working with trumpeter *Don CHERRY* (1936–95), he developed a free-form music based on connected but discontinuous melodic development, and split the jazz world when he performed at New York's Five Spot Café in 1959. After two West Coast albums, he was snapped up by

Free the album

Free jazz the music got its name from *Free Jazz* the album, recorded by Ornette in 1960 and played by two quartets, one on each channel. Each musician led the ensemble once as soloist, while the rest provided simultaneous comment. The only premeditated structure was the order of the solos and the ensemble horn parts that announced each solo. A revolutionary record, *Free Jazz* was the first free collective improvisation. Turbulent cacophony to some, pure freedom to others.

Atlantic, and within two years recorded six epic albums, with enough left over to fill another three released in later years.

Coleman accomplice Don Cherry, with his pocket trumpet.

1962 Actor Sean Connery is given the role of James Bond in the film *Dr. No*.

1963 The push-button telephone is launched in the U.S.

1964 In Copenhagen, the head of the Little Mermaid statue is sawn off.

Many critics and listeners failed to get beyond Coleman's harsh timbre or the lack of a recognizable harmonic or melodic structure—there was no piano to provide harmonic guidelines—but those who did discovered a musician of passion and considerable tenderness. Despite some apocalyptic album titles—*Change of the Century*, *The Shape of Jazz to Come*—much of the music was introspective and thoughtful, while pieces such as *Lonely Woman*, *Congeniality*, and *Peace* are little masterworks and now part of the standard repertoire. With his music now available on CD, it is possible to hear with greater clarity its collective and democratic intent, with the bass players in particular playing a major role in influencing the improvisations. But Coleman felt he was being ignored and, worse, willfully misunderstood, so in 1962 he retired from music for three years. When he returned he was playing violin and trumpet, and the

Free jazz

To define free jazz is all but impossible, as it is a collective term applied to numerous individual styles. But at its common core is the abandonment of the conventional harmonic, melodic, and rhythmic structures of jazz in favor of free personal expression. Coleman based his music on melodic improvisation. With no underlying chord sequence and no continuous melodic storyline to fall back on, Coleman (and the other soloists in his band) was out on his own, and succeeded or failed according to the strength of his melodic invention. Scary stuff, but capable in his hands of producing sheer beauty. Others were to take different routes to freedom.

Multi-instrumentalist with manuscript paper: Ornette Coleman refusing to be typecast.

controversy started up all over again, as his playing on these instruments was, if anything, even more abstract. Further controversies erupted over his work in the 1970s, but those can wait for another page.

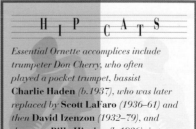

HIP CATS

Essential Ornette accomplices include trumpeter Don Cherry, who often played a pocket trumpet, bassist **Charlie Haden** *(b.1937), who was later replaced by* **Scott LaFaro** *(1936–61) and then* **David Izenzon** *(1932–79), and drummer* **Billy Higgins** *(b.1936), in turn replaced by* **Ed Blackwell** *(1929–92) and later,* **Charles Moffett** *(b.1929).*

ALL THAT JAZZ

Something Else, Tomorrow Is the Question (both OJC): the starters from 1958–59; *The Shape of Jazz to Come, Change of the Century, Free Jazz* (all Atlantic): the 1959–60 revolution; *Beauty Is a Rare Thing* (Rhino, 6 CDs): all the Atlantics from 1959–61; *At the Golden Circle, Stockholm* (Blue Note, 2 volumes): live in 1965.

1956 The design for Velcro is perfected by Swiss engineer Georges de Mertral.

1968 The epidural anesthetic is developed by scientists to ease pain in childbirth.

1972 American swimmer Mark Spitz wins a record 7 gold medals at the Munich Olympics.

1956~present

All Hands on Board

Cecil Taylor

Cecil Taylor demonstrates how to play the piano.

If Ornette Coleman had not existed, pianist Cecil TAYLOR (b.1929) would probably be considered the founding father of free jazz. Yet it was Taylor's fate to be in New York when Coleman arrived in the fall of 1959, with the result that his career was eclipsed for several years. But whereas Coleman remained accessible with his one-touch melodic invention, Taylor pursued jazz abstraction to its farthest degree. Whatever else his music might be, it is not an easy listen. Be warned!

Taylor was trained as a classical pianist, studying piano and theory at the New England Conservatory in the early 1950s. His interest in jazz was late in developing, and it was not until he played a six-week residency at the Five Spot Café in New York in 1956—the first jazz musician to do so—that he became known on the jazz scene. At first his music was rooted in traditional forms, though his interpretations were highly individual, but by the early 1960s Taylor was out on his own. Playing without any kind of conventional jazz rhythm, Taylor's music became totally abstract and non-tonal. What harmonic signposts he stabbed out with his insistent left hand were soon swamped by a swirl of atonal, chromatic clusters of notes produced with open palms, fists, and elbows as well as the traditional ten

Cecil Taylor in full flight. He can prove exhausting to listen to, but the impression of superhuman energy resonates through every performance.

1987 Prince releases his extraordinary double album *Sign O' The Times*.

1988 Stephen Hawking's book *A Brief History of Time* is published and reaches the top of the bestseller list, although it's difficult to find anyone who has read it.

1992 Bill Cosby becomes America's highest-paid entertainer, taking first place from pop band New Kids on the Block.

ALL THAT JAZZ

CECIL TAYLOR—*Jazz Advance* (Blue Note)—1956 beginnings; *The World of Cecil Taylor* (Candid)—a 1960 quartet set; *Unit Structures* (Blue Note); *Garden* (hat ART—two volumes)—solo piano from 1981; *Live in Bologna* (Leo)—live quintet set from 1987.

MARILYN CRISPELL—*For Coltrane* (Leo)—1987 solo set; *Overlapping Hands: Eight Segments* (FMP)—a 1990 duo with Irène Schweizer.

MYRA MELFORD—*Jump* (Enemy); *Alive in the House of Saints* (hat ART)—live Jump.

IRÈNE SCHWEIZER—*Piano Solo* (Intakt—two volumes).

Whatever comments have been made about Taylor's music, no one denies his undoubted technical expertise.

fingers in order to overcome the limitations of the piano's fixed pitch. There is no thematic development, rather a series of statements progressing from one to another with a fierce internal logic. Often played at high volume and ferocious speeds, his music was and remains tumultuous, orgasmic even.

To witness a Taylor performance is to participate in an endurance test—for pianist and audience alike—as Taylor can play unaccompanied for two to three hours, his brilliant technique aided by enormous stamina and delivered with a percussive, physical attack. Not surprisingly, Taylor's music achieved massive critical acclaim but a minute audience, for many found his work closer to the European avant-garde than anything they recognized in jazz. The Art Tatum of free jazz, Taylor remains uncompromising, unrelenting, and totally individual.

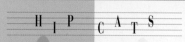

HIP CATS

Those few pianists who managed to take Taylor's work on board and run with it are mainly women. Swiss-born **Irène Schweizer** *(b.1941) is closest to him in style, although less percussive, while* **Marilyn Crispell** *(b.1947) owes as much to John Coltrane in her sometimes spiritual approach. Most accessible of the three is* **Myra Melford** *(b.1960), who merges passages of free expression with infectious melodic hooks, notably on the funky* Jump. *Whatever their differences, all three have taken from Taylor an extraordinary technique and a powerful performing presence.*

1960 The film *Ben Hur* receives a record ten Oscars.

1963 In Britain, the BBC withdraws its ban on the mention of sex, religion, politics, and royalty on comedy shows.

1964 The soldier doll called G.I. Joe (U.S.) /Action Man (U.K.) appears in stores for the first time.

1960~1970
Freedom Now!
The New Thing in Jazz

The new jazz ushered in by Ornette Coleman fell on receptive ears in New York, for it coincided with the explosion of black politics started by the civil rights movement. The freedom sought by the black community in political and social life was mirrored by the freedom sought by black jazz musicians in new forms of musical expression, and so hand in glove, the two revolutions —political and musical—advanced throughout the 1960s.

Civil rights march on Washington, August 28, 1963, with Martin Luther King (front row, second from left). Jazz musicians joined the fray and expressed a musical revolution.

ESP-Disk

The house label for the new jazz was ESP-Disk, formed in New York in 1962 by Bernard Stollman, a music lawyer used to handling musicians' business affairs. Bizarrely, he owned no record player, had never bought a record, and knew little about jazz itself. He attended every one of the October concerts and later recorded many of those involved. Such was the revolutionary nature of the music that ESP's second record—Albert Ayler's *Spiritual Unity*—was recorded in mono, as the engineer could not believe it was anything other than a demo! Stollman wrote the liner notes in English and Esperanto—ESP was short for Esperanto; Stollman was involved in the international language movement, and the label's first record was a sing-along in Esperanto! Poor at publicity and appalling at payment, Stollman recorded the cream of the avant-garde until the label collapsed in 1974. Most notorious record? Try Ayler's *Bells*, pressed on one side only of clear red plastic.

I n true democratic form, this new wave of musicians had no leaders but numerous participants. Chief among them was trumpeter *Bill DIXON* (b.1925), who organized a series of six concerts in October 1964 that were soon referred to with full pun intended as The October Revolution. Only a maximum of 65 people per night witnessed these historic concerts and their four successors in December, held in the Cellar Café off Broadway, but the list of largely unknowns who participated— drummers *Milford GRAVES* (b.1941) and *Rashied ALI* (b.1935), pianists *Cecil TAYLOR* (b.1933) and *Paul BLEY* (b.1932), saxophonists *Archie SHEPP* (b.1937) and *John TCHICAI* (b.1936), Ornette's bassist

1966 British businessman Freddie Laker launches Laker Airways, specializing in cheap vacation flights.

1969 Woodstock music festival takes place near Bethel, New York. It runs for 3 days and attracts 300,000 people.

1970 The New English Bible sells a million copies in its first week of publication.

ALL THAT JAZZ

BILL DIXON—*November 1981* (Soul Note)—a late but perfect example of this trumpeter's art.
MILFORD GRAVES—*Percussion Ensemble* (ESP).
JAZZ COMPOSER'S ORCHESTRA—*Communications* (JCOA)—a new-wave cast of thousands from 1968, most notably Cecil Taylor and Don Cherry.
NEW YORK ART QUARTET—*New York Art Quartet* (ESP)—Rudd, Graves, and others in 1964.

Free drumming

While it has been the saxophonists of the avant-garde who have attracted most attention, and therefore get two pages to themselves shortly, the drummers joined in the revolution as well. Sunny Murray (b.1937), Andrew Cyrille (b.1939), Milford Graves (b.1941), Rashied Ali (b.1935), and Dennis Charles (1933–98), most of whom played with either Cecil Taylor or Albert Aylor, all freed jazz drumming from any timekeeping role, joining in the collective improvisation by accenting freely and making full use of the range of the drum set's different timbres and pitches. Graves played most free, introducing bells, gongs, and shakers, and concentrating not on rhythm but on the range of different sounds the drums can make.

David IZENZON (1932–79), trombonist *Roswell RUDD* (b.1935), the Sun Ra Arkestra (see p. 102), and many more—defined the avant-garde of their day. Out of these concerts grew the Jazz Composers Guild, a short-lived cooperative venture formed by Dixon, which aimed to promote free jazz performances independently of existing nightclubs and booking agents, and the Jazz Composer's Orchestra, led by *Michael MANTLER* (b.1943) and *Carla BLEY* (b.1938), of whom more later.

The importance of the October Revolution and its ripple effect on the wider musical community cannot be overestimated, for it marked the emergence of free jazz as a mature movement, but life on the outer reaches rarely has much appeal for a mass audience, whose racial awareness was more easily tapped by a James Brown or later a Sly Stone, and little of this earth-shaking music achieved wide circulation. No one generic term sums up what was played, but what all participants held in common was a willingness to experiment, stripping away the restraints of structure, harmony, and melody in a search for absolute personal freedom of expression. The man who personifies this arduous journey is John Coltrane.

Carla Bley, one of the most important jazz composers of the last thirty years.

1957 Jack Kerouac's novel *On the Road* shocks Middle America with its portrayal of sex and drug culture.

1958 The skateboard is invented by Bill and Mark Richards in California.

1959 Tibetan spiritual leader the Dalai Lama arrives in India seeking political asylum.

1956~1967

A Love Supreme
John Coltrane

Let me jump straight in here: John Coltrane: A Crash Course *would not be long enough to contain all that needs to be said about this extraordinary saxophonist, for in every way* COLTRANE *(1926–67) is one of the most important jazz musicians of all time, and one of the most revered. Alongside Armstrong, Parker, Davis, and Coleman, he is one of the major innovators of jazz, whose playing transformed the jazz landscape. Not that he is always an easy listen.*

Coltrane played soprano sax increasingly from 1960.

A brief career résumé. After an early career in R&B bands, Coltrane played bop with Gillespie and others before joining Miles Davis in 1955–57. After spending 1957 with Monk, he returned to Miles between 1958 and 1960, playing on *Kind of Blue* and other records. From 1956 he recorded many sessions under his own name, but only in 1960 was he ready to front his own group.

In many ways Coltrane was not a natural leader, taking time to find his voice. *Giant Steps* was the turning point, the title track marking the high water mark of bop as Coltrane steams through the chord changes at the rate of two per bar. Brilliant, but for him a creative dead end, in contrast to the simpler structures of *Naima*, reflecting the modal music he was pioneering with Miles.

ALL THAT JAZZ

Blue Train (Blue Note): a strong session from 1957; *John Coltrane and the Jazz Giants* (Prestige): early Coltrane, 1956–58; *Giant Steps* (Atlantic): 1959 masterpiece; *The Heavyweight Champion* (Atlantic/Rhino, 7 CDs): complete Coltrane on Atlantic, 1959–61; *The Complete 1961 Village Vanguard Recordings* (4 CDs): seminal live recording; *Coltrane*: the classic quartet in 1962; *Ballads*: in a quiet mood; *A Love Supreme, The Major Works* (2 CDs): includes *Ascension* (all Impulse).

1961 The birth control pill is launched in the U.S.

1964 The film première of *A Hard Day's Night* causes a huge traffic jam in central London as thousands of fans arrive hoping to catch sight of the Beatles.

1968 Rock guitarist Jimi Hendrix soars up the charts with his albums *Axis: Bold As Love* and *Electric Ladyland*.

With the formation of his quartet in 1960 Coltrane acquired the perfect voice. Tentatively at first, he laid down a body of work that still confounds all those who hear it today. Ignore the technicalities of modes and overtones and false fingering or how he constructed his "sheets of sound," just listen to the music. Everything Coltrane played—on tenor or soprano, and at every speed from funereal to ecstatic— he played as an act of catharsis, his deepening spirituality imbuing each track with emotional fervor. Two albums stand out—*A Love Supreme* from 1964, a four-part paean to God and by inference all supreme deities, and *Ascension* from 1965, a collective improvisation far freer than Coleman's groundbreaking *Free Jazz*, to which it is erroneously compared. *A Love Supreme* is generally regarded as Coltrane's masterpiece, largely because of its approachability, but it was *Ascension* that highlighted the freedom Coltrane sought in his work.

Where Coltrane might have progressed to is an open question, for in July 1967 he died of liver failure. While it is possible to sideline Coleman and free jazz as an artistic dead end, it is impossible to ignore Coltrane, for even at his most extreme, he lies at the very heart of jazz, influencing every saxophonist and most other jazz musicians ever since. To put it bluntly, if you can't cope with Coltrane, you can't cope with jazz.

Elvin Jones, the Coltrane Quartet's brilliant drummer; the two players struck sparks!

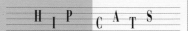

HIP CATS

*The classic Coltrane Quartet was formed in 1960 with pianist **McCoy Tyner** (b.1938) and drummer **Elvin Jones** (b.1927), bassist **Jimmy Garrison** (1934–76) joining in 1961. Other musicians, notably **Eric Dolphy** (1928–64) on bass clarinet, were added for live performances. Saxophonist **Pharoah Sanders** (b.1940) and drummer **Rashied Ali** (b.1935) joined the group in 1965, followed by Coltrane's pianist wife **Alice** (b.1937) in 1966, by which time Jones and Tyner had left. The classic quartet was a powerhouse, with Tyner keeping time with splashy runs of notes and heart-stopping chords, Garrison laying down walking bass lines or persistent drones, and Jones playing dense polyrhythmic lines of great complexity that buoyed up the leader. As McCoy Tyner remarked, they worked "like four pistons in an engine." Anything but a traditional rhythm section.*

TAMA
ELVIN JONES
Jazz Machine

1962 Pop artist Roy Lichtenstein holds his first one-man show in New York City.

1972 Bobby Fischer becomes the first American to win the world chess title, defeating grand master Boris Spassky, at Reykjavik, Iceland.

1978 Louise Brown, the world's first test-tube baby, is born in Britain.

1962~present

Saxophone Extremes

Sanders, Shepp, Ayler

Albert Ayler: "It's not about notes any more. It's about feelings." The second wave of new wave players showed a ferocity that has never been equaled.

Where might John Coltrane's music have led him? One possible answer lies in the careers of three of the next generation of saxophonists—Pharoah Sanders, Archie Shepp, and Albert Ayler— who ignited jazz during the 1960s. All three were heavily influenced by Coltrane (and to a lesser extent by Coleman, too), and it was through his patronage that they recorded for Impulse, the most important record label of the avant-garde—"The New Wave of Jazz is on Impulse!" was its claim. Yet all three showed clearly what the limits of freedom might be.

Pharoah SANDERS (b.1940) started out in R&B, but on his arrival in New York in 1962 quickly linked up with the free jazz scene, and was pulled into Coltrane's group in 1965 as an equally impassioned counterpoint to the leader. His harsh, shrieking improvisations were at the extremes of jazz, but after Coltrane's death he pulled back, as if exhausted by his efforts, and was soon turning out hippyish anthems about freedom and the creator's master plan. By the 1980s a generation of clubbers were dancing to his music.

Archie SHEPP (b.1937) traced an equally interesting trajectory, from the politics of Black Consciousness—he likened his saxophone to a machine gun, which he no doubt intended to use—toward conserving the jazz heritage: "Worse than a romantic, I'm a sentimentalist." Shepp was always less abstract than the other new wave saxophonists, despite playing on the album *Ascension*, and by the late 1970s he was wearing a three-piece tweed suit and turning out loving recreations of gospel and blues songs.

1987 In San Francisco the first television commercials for condoms are broadcast.

1993 American rock musician Prince replaces his name with a symbol, and becomes the Artist Formerly Known As Prince.

1996 In the U.S., same-sex marriages are prohibited under the new Defense of Marriage Act.

Eric Dolphy

Eric Dolphy (1928–64) stands out from the other saxophonists of his day, both for his multi-instrumental talents—he played alto sax, flute, clarinet, and bass clarinet—and for his equal facility at whatever he attempted. He is linked with the new wave because of his performance opposite Ornette on *Free Jazz* and his role as foil to John Coltrane at the Village Vanguard in 1961, but he was a much more orthodox player than those links would suggest, and was in his element working in the various Charlie Mingus bands. *Out to Lunch!*, a 1964 session with an almost-free rhythm section, touching all the modernist bases but flying above them all. His early death robbed jazz of one of its finest creators.

Eric Dolphy, collaborator with the stars Coltrane, Mingus, and Coleman included.

ALL THAT JAZZ

ALBERT AYLER—*Spiritual Unity, Spirits Rejoice* (both ESP); *In Greenwich Village* (Impulse).
ERIC DOLPHY—*Out to Lunch!* (Blue Note).
PHAROAH SANDERS—*Tauhid, Karma* (both Impulse); *Journey to the One* (Evidence), with clubland classic *You've Got to Have Freedom*.
ARCHIE SHEPP—*Fire Music* (MCA); *New Thing at Newport* (Impulse); *Goin' Home, Trouble in Mind* (both Steeplechase): Shepp and pianist Horace Parlan explore gospel and blues songs respectively.

Albert AYLER (1936–70) was greeted as either charlatan or messiah, and controversy raged throughout his short career. Wild, demonic, and with a raw, emotional range encompassing tenderness and brutality, Ayler harked back to New Orleans marching bands and blues vocals, yet never sounded anything other than contemporary.

"It's about feelings," he said, although one poet expressed the feeling that his music was like screaming "fuck" in New York's St. Patrick's Cathedral. Coltrane requested that Ayler play at his funeral, along with Coleman, but as the '60s played themselves out in the assassinations of hope and the jungles of Vietnam, Ayler retreated from the edge and mellowed into gospel-tinged R&B. His

mysterious death in 1970—missing for 20 days, then fished out of New York's East River—was probably suicide; it marked the end of an era, and was, in its tragic way, symptomatic of the death of new wave extremism. It was fun, and fiery, while it lasted.

Archie Shepp: revolutionary, or curator of jazz?

1951 Photographs of giant footsteps suggesting the existence of an abominable snowman are taken by British mountaineer Eric Shipton.

1968 Stanley Kubrick's extraordinary sci-fi film *2001: A Space Odyssey* is released.

1976 The *Viking II* spacecraft lands on Utopia Plains on the planet Mars.

1954~1993

We Come from Saturn

Sun Ra

The Heliocentric Worlds of Sun Ra, classic adventurousness from 1965.

It would be tempting to suggest that after the raging intensity and heartfelt passion of the previous few pages, Sun Ra (1914–93) comes on as the comic turn, the vaudeville figure in a funny costume who thought he came from Saturn and performed odd songs about Egypt and all corners of the solar system with a raggle-taggle band of musicians romping away behind him. But that would be to confuse surface with substance, to ignore the very hard core of self-belief that kept him and his remarkable Arkestra on the road for almost forty years.

Sun Ra was a product of the big band era, producing arrangements for the Fletcher Henderson band and playing small-group swing in Chicago clubs in the 1940s. But Ra's arrangements were always slightly oblique, slightly different from what anyone else could hear or play, and he was soon out on his own, running a number of small groups that by 1954 had evolved into an octet. The Arkestra was born, its name constantly varying, its personnel revolving around a hard core of adventurous, dedicated musicians, notably Pat Patrick and John Gilmore, who would stay with Ra for life. The Arkestra lived, worked, and endlessly rehearsed together, the fruits of their labors issued on Ra's own Saturn label, complete with hand-painted album covers and erratic distribution

Legions of first-class musicians have played with the Arkestra in its forty-year history. Preeminent among them are three saxophonists: **Pat Patrick** *(b.1929),* **Marshall Allen** *(b.1924), and* **John Gilmore** *(1931–95), whose tenor playing is said to have influenced Coltrane (a rare role reversal there). Among the alumni are violinist* **Billy Bang** *(b.1947), trombonist* **Julian Priester** *(b.1935), and drummer* **Clifford Jarvis** *(b.1941)—although instrumentation is irrelevant, as noted on the cover notes to* Space Is the Place: *"as all Marines are riflemen, all members of the Arkestra are percussionists."*

1978 The craze for "Space Invaders," the first arcade video game, takes off worldwide.

1982 Michael Jackson's album *Thriller* is promoted with a 10-minute feature film directed by John Landis.

1991 Crop circles become a worldwide phenomenon, particularly in Britain, Germany, and across the U.S.

methods—records were often sold at the end of a gig to raise cash to get the band to its next venue! At first the Arkestra played a wayward, sentimental swing music, but by the 1960s it was orbiting the outer reaches of Planet Jazz, participating in the 1964 October Revolution and, between 1966 and 1972, playing a regular Monday-night residency at Slug's bar in New York that defined the entire history of jazz, from swing to free and beyond, in lengthy three-hour-plus gigs. The band wore extravagant costumes and was joined on stage by dancers and singers, parading around the bar chanting about traveling the spaceways or flying to Jupiter. Ra had always been interested in new technology, and in 1955 had been one of the first jazz

Somewhere in the firmament he is playing still...

musicians to buy and record with an electric piano. By the late 1960s he was using Mini-Moog synthesizers to create washes of electronic sound, matched in intensity by the honking and squealing of his frontline hornmen, who were supported by the entire Arkestra on percussion.

As the Arkestra aged, it inevitably slowed down, burning up like a satellite as it hit Earth's atmosphere. By the 1980s it had reverted to its swing origins, space age campery notwithstanding, and was even playing Disney tunes to great effect. But individual stars still burned brightly on stage, and few devotees will forget those memorable nights when the Arkestra played its collective heart out on some ill-equipped stage at the back end of nowhere. Unforgettable, and much missed.

ALL THAT JAZZ

Evidence Records is slowly excavating the Saturn catalog and issuing it on CD. Any of the Evidence CDs—15 in all to date, plus a two-CD set of Arkestra singles—are worth listening to, especially *Jazz in Silhouette* from 1958, *The Magic City* from 1965, and *Atlantis* from 1967–69. The title tracks of the latter two albums rival Coltrane's *Ascension* in their scope and grandeur.
The Heliocentric Worlds of Sun Ra (ESP, 2 volumes): Ra at his most adventurous in 1965; *Space Is the Place* (Impulse), from 1972; *St. Louis Blues* (Improvising Artists): solo Ra on piano in 1977; *Second Star to the Right* (Leo): Ra's tribute to Disney (and why not?); *Sunrise in Different Dimensions* (hat ART): Ra reviewing his musical heritage.

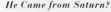

He Came from Saturn?

Born on May 22, 1914, in Birmingham, Alabama, Herman Poole Blount always claimed he was Sun Ra (or many variant spellings) and came from Saturn. Not as unlikely as it sounds, for as a descendant of slaves, his name was a product not of lineage but of ownership, so if others could name him, so could he, and select his birthplace, too. And who are we to disprove him?

1972 In Rome, Michelangelo's Pietà is damaged by a deranged man with a hammer.

1977 Powerful 12-hour television drama series *Roots* gets top ratings in the U.S.

1984 In California a security guard shoots dead 20 people in McDonald's because he "hates Mondays."

1966~present

Great Black Music
The Art Ensemble of Chicago

From New York to Chicago. Or from the hothouse atmosphere of racial passions to the free-jazz abstractions of the Association for the Advancement of Creative Musicians and its legion participants. There in the Windy City, the cooperative re-creation and distillation of black music gave birth to the theatrical and eclectic Art Ensemble of Chicago, still in operation thirty years later.

Joseph Jarman, multi-instrumentalist, was a mainstay of the Art Ensemble who played every conceivable member of the saxophone family.

The AACM

The Association for the Advancement of Creative Musicians was formed in Chicago in 1965 by pianist and composer Muhal Richard Abrams (b.1930). It grew out of his Experimental Band, one of the first free-jazz ensembles, founded in 1961, and is devoted to the advancement of black avant-garde jazz. The AACM is a non-profit cooperative which in its many ventures has been a hotbed for such artists as the Art Ensemble, composer and reedsman Anthony Braxton (b.1945), trumpeter Leo Smith (b.1941), and violinist Leroy Jenkins (b.1932), and it remains one of the major catalysts in the development of a black classical music called jazz.

The Art Ensemble grew out of a group led by *Roscoe MITCHELL*, and by 1968 was a four-piece with *Lester BOWIE*, *Malachi FAVORS*, and *Joseph JARMAN*. Their work was slow to be accepted, so in 1969 they moved to Paris for 18 months. Paris has always been a refuge for black musicians and usually a city conducive to jazz, but after *les événements de mai* it was in a rather conservative mood, and oddly resistant to experimental jazz. Now officially known as the Art Ensemble of Chicago, the band struggled at first, but a steady stream of records and live performances began to find them an audience. By now they were a five-piece,

1985 The Church of England approves the ordination of women as deacons.

1986 20-year-old Mike Tyson becomes the youngest world heavyweight boxing champion in history.

1987 The grunge movement begins in Seattle with the musical experimentation of Nirvana and other bands, such as Mudhoney.

The Art Ensemble, dressed for action.

H I P   C A T S

Art Ensemble members **Lester Bowie** *(b.1941) on trumpet, reedsmen* **Joseph Jarman** *(b.1937) and* **Roscoe Mitchell** *(b.1940), bass player* **Malachi Favors** *(b.1937), and later addition drummer* **Famadou Don Moye** *(b.1946) are all considerable improvisers and performers in their own right. Trumpeter Bowie stands out for his mixture of blurred runs and single bell-like notes blasting into the upper register, but the fierce integrity of both Jarman and Mitchell are essential to the whole project. And as with the Arkestra, all Ensemble members are percussionists, playing a range of bells, drums, and many other instruments in their search for sonic possibilities.*

with the addition in 1970 of drummer *Famadou Don* MOYE, and by the time they returned to the U.S. their identity was established. Moving imperceptibly from lengthy free abstraction into pieces drawn from across the jazz tradition, the Art Ensemble is in every sense theatrical—Bowie wearing his white lab technician's coat, the others in African face paint and costumes, all performing on a stage littered with percussion and ethnic instruments and a range of horns and whistles. Silence is an important part of their repertoire, and they conjure up music that ranges from the surreal through the abstract to the absurd, keeping their feet on the ground with some hard-hitting bop, a reminder that they treat all their music with equal weight and seriousness.

Not for nothing do they celebrate "Great Black Music—Ancient to the Future," for theirs is a

ALL THAT JAZZ

MUHAL RICHARD ABRAMS— *One Line, Two Views* (New World): a large-scale work from 1995.
ART ENSEMBLE OF CHICAGO—*Tutankhamen* (Black Lion): early days in 1969; *Live* (Delmark) and *Urban Bushmen* (ECM, 2 CDs): live in 1972 and 1980.
LESTER BOWIE'S BRASS FANTASY—*Serious Fun* (DIW).
ANTHONY BRAXTON— *Dortmund* (Quartet) *1976* (hat ART); *Creative Orchestra* (Köln) *1978* (hat ART, 2 CDs).
LEROY JENKINS—*Urban Blues* (Black Saint).

timeless music. However, even time slows down eventually, and by the late 1980s they were often just going through their paces, Bowie setting off on solo projects with his good-time bands. But this is to judge them harshly: the Art Ensemble was always a live band, their virtuosic performances as much visual as sonic. For 30 years they have played wonderful music.

1969 Beatle John Lennon and his wife, artist and writer Yoko Ono, stage a seven-day "bed-in" as a protest against violence and war.

1973 The comedy series M*A*S*H* and Depression-era series *The Waltons* première on American television.

1975 The first pop video is shown in Britain, on the BBC's *Top of the Pops*—Queen's *Bohemian Rhapsody*.

1960~1994

Jazz in Exile
The South African Exiles

Waiting for the Rain, a fine example of Hugh Masekela's burnished trumpet tones.

With the honorable exceptions of Reinhardt and Grappelli, we've so far stayed close to the U.S., begetter of and sustenance to the jazz world. But by the 1950s jazz had spread far and wide, its universal language finding a resonance in many different countries. In South Africa it took root in an apartheid society that outdid the worst excesses of the American South. Racial prejudice was enshrined in law, forbidding mixed-race assembly and performance, but out of this barren, censored land came music that was to have worldwide implications.

The Sharpeville massacre in March 1960 and subsequent clampdown on black South Africans sent the two most important jazz groups into exile. The Jazz Epistles, an all-black sextet including *Dollar BRAND* (b.1934) on piano and *Hugh MASEKELA* (b.1939) on trumpet, played "township bebop," a bop and African *kwela* mix: in 1960 they recorded *Verse I*, the first album by a black South African jazz group. The Blue Notes, founded in 1963 by pianist *Chris McGREGOR* (1936–90), were a township band unique in being multiracial.

Their combined impact on the jazz world was extraordinary. Masekela became an ambassador for African jazz, touring the world and campaigning against apartheid. Abdullah Ibrahim (as Dollar Brand

1986 Paul Simon releases the African-inspired album *Graceland* featuring Ladysmith Black Mambazo and is blacklisted for breaking the U.N. boycott of South Africa.

1990 Soviet citizens are permitted to own land for the first time since 1922.

1994 Edvard Munch's famous painting *The Scream* is stolen from Oslo's National Art Museum as part of an antiabortion campaign.

The trumpet from God

Or from Bishop Trevor Huddleston, near enough to God in many people's eyes for his work in South Africa and later as president of the Anti-Apartheid Movement. In the 1950s Huddleston gave Masekela his first trumpet and encouraged him in his musical career. Masekela never looked back.

Yes Please! The Brotherhood of Breath live at Angoulême in 1981.

became) played with Duke Ellington and later most of the avant-garde, before returning to his African roots. Still touring regularly in the 1990s, Ibrahim's mix of incantatory chants, joyous township rhythms, and jazz *à la* Monk has taken solo jazz performance to new heights.

The Blue Notes made a different impact. In 1966 they played at Copenhagen's Montmartre Club, a focus for new wave musicians, and from then on fused their African music with free jazz. Evolving in 1970 into the wondrous, anarchic Brotherhood of Breath big band, they bore strongly on the development of European free jazz (of which more later), their complex rhythmic structures and collective improvising influencing a generation of European jazz musicians from across the spectrum.

What these and other South African jazz musicians brought with them into exile was an exuberance of rhythm and melody that shook up the staid world of European jazz in particular, exposing insular musicians to a different continent's musical heritage. Although few lived to see it, the ending of apartheid and the election of Nelson Mandela as South African president in 1994 was everything they had worked for.

Police action in Soweto township, May 1986: oppression as always a powerful stimulus to jazz.

ALL THAT JAZZ

BLUE NOTES—*Live in South Africa 1964* (Ogun).
BROTHERHOOD OF BREATH—*Live at Willisau* (Ogun): an all-star cast live in 1973.
ABDULLAH IBRAHIM—*African Piano* (Japo): solo piano from 1969; *African Marketplace* (Discovery), *Water from an Ancient Well* (Tiptoe), *African River* (Enja): fronting various-sized groups from 1979–89.
THE JAZZ EPISTLES—*Jazz in Africa* (Camden): includes *Verse 1*.
HUGH MASEKELA—*Liberation* (Jive); *Waiting for the Rain* (Jive Afrika, LP only).

1962 Coffee-producing countries form the International Coffee Organization in an attempt to regulate production and stabilize coffee prices.

1962 Brazil, without the injured Pele, retain the Soccer World Cup that they had first won in Sweden in 1958.

1962 Pope John XXIII insists that Latin remain the language of the Roman Catholic Church.

1962~1964
Getz Gets Bossa
Stan Getz

Rio's Sugar Loaf Mountain.

The last kick of cool jazz before it was swamped by the heady wave of the 1960s came not from the West Coast but the southern seas, from the beaches of Rio de Janeiro. There a mixture of samba—the rhythm of carnival—and cool jazz produced the gently lilting rhythms and quiet tones of bossa nova, which sprang to world prominence and put jazz albums and singles onto the Billboard *charts. The unlikely recipient of this fame was an aggressive saxophonist called Stan Getz.*

We've met *Stan GETZ* (1927–91) before, as one of the Four Brothers saxophone frontline in the Woody Herman Second Herd of 1947. For much of the 1950s he recorded some fine cool jazz albums with the likes of Gerry Mulligan and Oscar Peterson, and might have plodded along without much impact had it not been for an encounter with guitarist *Charlie BYRD* (b.1925) in 1961. Byrd played Getz some South American music, Getz liked it, and—never having visited the place, let alone played its music—recorded

> ### ALL THAT JAZZ
>
> **STAN GETZ**—*Jazz Samba*—includes *Desafinado*; *Big Band Bossa Nova, Jazz Samba Encore, Getz/Gilberto*—includes *The Girl from Ipanema, Getz Au Go Go*—Getz swings bossa nova, all from 1962–64, *The Girl from Ipanema* (4 CDs)—complete collected bossa nova (all Verve); *Pure Getz, Blue Skies* (both Concord), *Anniversary* (Emarcy)—prime Getz from the 1980s.

Stan Getz, unlikely though it looks, captured the warm allure of Ipanema. Getz made a highly profitable fusion of Latin American music in his most famous album, *Jazz Samba*.

1962 The Cuban missile crisis brings Cuba and the U.S. to the brink of war.

1963 Nude screen tests are held for the film *Four for Texas* and Ursula Andress wins the main role.

1964 Pulitzer prizes are canceled with a committee announcement that no fiction, drama, or music has been good enough to merit an award.

Bossa Nova

Literally, "new wave," a form of Brazilian music rare for being invented by one person—Antonio Carlos Jobim (1927–94), who devised the distinct rhythm. He wrote both *Desafinado* (*Out of Tune*) and *A Garota de Ipanema* (the proverbial *Girl from...*), and was later haunted by the many and appalling cover versions of the song. Bossa nova developed in Rio de Janeiro's chic beach neighborhood of Ipanema by day and the clubs of Copacabana by night, before being taken up by jazz musicians and given worldwide acclaim. Getz remarked that he soon "got bored with it, but it paid for my kids to go through college." We remain unsure what the unnamed girl got out of it.

a set of unprepared bossa nova pieces in February 1962. The resultant album, *Jazz Samba*, went onto the *Billboard* record charts, where it stayed for 70 weeks, and the main track, *Desafinado*, hit the *Billboard* Hot 100 singles chart. If that was not enough, a collaboration in 1964 between Getz and guitarist *João Gilberto* (b.1931) on the album *Getz/ Gilberto* produced *The Girl from Ipanema*, sung in deadpan English by João's wife *Astrud* (b.1940). That single reached No. 5 on the Hot 100 and stayed on the charts for 12 weeks.

Astrud Gilberto, the cool vocal counterpoint to Getz's saxophone.

Getz was no rock'n'roll star, despite a lifestyle fueled by drink and drugs. Despairing of the twin onslaught on jazz by free jazz and rock music, he retired for the rest of the decade. But in that brief two years, Getz brought to jazz an audience it might never have gained, and opened jazz up to a host of musical influences from around the world. And we all just loved that song.

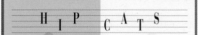

HIP CATS

Pre-Getz, the man who did much to popularize bossa nova in jazz was guitarist and composer **Laurindo Almeida** *(1918–95). An alumnus of the Stan Kenton Band from 1947–49, Almeida worked on movie soundtracks. His quartet recordings with alto saxophonist* **Bud Shank** *(b.1926) in 1953 and 1958 introduced the Brazilian guitar to jazz. "We didn't call it bossa nova then, but that's what it was," he remarked later. Other big Brazilian names: guitarist* **Gilberto Gil** *(b.1942) has concentrated on the African element in Brazilian music, and has often fallen foul of the authorities for his protest songs, while singer* **Milton Nascimento** *(b.1942) has worked with saxophonist Wayne Shorter and others.*

1958~1980

Another Kind of Freedom

Bill Evans

The classic jazz trio: piano, bass, and drums.

Although there were many fine pianists around at the end of the 1950s, Thelonious Monk and Bud Powell cast shadows over them all, their bop style of fragmented right-hand melodies and random, spiky left-hand chords influencing most other pianists. With one exception: a quiet, frail man named Bill EVANS (1929–80), whose sensitive, expressive touch stood him in complete contrast to the often cacophonous sound of bop or free jazz. Not that Evans was conservative—he was no light-fingered cocktail pianist—but on the principle that less equals more, the minimalism of Bill produced one of the finest pianists in jazz.

Evans took time to find his style, for he was exploring a new language for the piano using modes: as we've already seen, he played on Miles's seminal *Kind of Blue*. Indeed *Peace Piece*, from his own album *Everybody Digs Bill Evans*, was the prototype of *Flamenco Sketches*, and Evans wrote *Blues in Green*, despite Miles taking the credit. But Evans's favored medium was not the sextet but the classic trio of piano,

bass, and drums, and in 1959 he formed one of the finest examples. The drum chair was taken by *Paul MOTIAN* (b.1931), an experienced drummer at home with most styles, but star of the show was bass player *Scott LAFARO* (1936–61), who was simultaneously playing free jazz with Ornette Coleman. LaFaro was hideously versatile, delivering solo lines a bop pianist or guitarist might attempt, often in the difficult higher register, and, in partnership with Motian, playing every rhythm from straightahead bop to almost free. Together the three were an ideal unit, for they displayed uncanny interplay and an instinctive rapport with one another's contributions. No one had primacy, for each was simultaneously soloist and accompanist combined, and they played

1978 Television reporter Max Robinson becomes the first black to anchor network news.

1980 Singer Tom Waits is awarded £2.5 million in damages after a television commercial imitates his voice.

1986 America celebrates the 100th anniversary of the Statue of Liberty.

with perfect melodic and rhythmic freedom, judging its limits to perfection. In their hands, the jazz trio became a three-way spontaneous conversation.

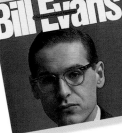

Bill Evans: his one night at the Village Vanguard has now become legendary.

Yet it is easy to miss the revolutionary nature of this trio, for Evans's innate lyricism and sheer beauty casts a lustrous sheen over every piece. He might have

Bill Evans presents a studious side to the outside world.

played quietly, but he was never cool, his relaxed intimacy hiding considerable compositional and improvisational sophistication. What they might have gone on to achieve beyond two studio albums and a live set from New York's Village Vanguard Club (part of which is on *Waltz for Debby*) remains unknown, for LaFaro was killed in a car accident in July 1961, aged 25. Evans was immensely distressed, and although he established a new trio and continued to work and record, he was never able to regain the heights achieved when LaFaro played glorious bass.

Overdubbing

The introduction of magnetic tape in the late 1940s opened up many possibilities, although jazz musicians were slow to avail themselves of the new technology. At first, studio trickery was restricted to removing obvious mistakes, but in 1951 pianist Lennie Tristano pioneered the use of overdubbing, that is, recording a solo track ("track" here meaning layer of sound—not to be confused with "tracks" on an album) and then accompanying himself on further tracks which were then combined with the original. Bill Evans was the first to overdub an entire album, recording the three tracks of *Conversations with Myself* in 1963. Charlie Mingus used the same principle on *The Black Saint and the Sinner Lady* in the same year, overdubbing the alto saxophone line as well as making 50 other alterations. Such tinkering hardly equals the 550 hours of studio time spent four years later on the Beatles' *Sergeant Pepper*, but only one jazz musician has ever gone to similar lengths: predictably enough Miles Davis, aided and abetted for hours by Columbia producer Teo Macero.

1965 The Hare Krishna movement is founded in the U.S. by ex-accountant A.C. Bhaktivedanta.

1965 British director David Lean begins filming *Doctor Zhivago*, based on the Nobel Prize-winning novel of the same name by Boris Pasternak.

1966 Barbara Jordan becomes the first black woman to win a seat in the Texas Senate.

1965~1968
Time—No Changes
Acoustic Miles Davis

What, more Miles? Haven't we heard enough of him by now? Well, according to taste, no; and there's more to look forward to. Or yes, but you can't ignore the fact that six times in postwar jazz, Miles has rewritten the history books. So although we've already placed him at the Birth of the Cool, made him a major hard bop player with his first classic quintet, set him up with arranger Gil Evans for those three sumptuous studio sets, and named him as catalyst for modal jazz, he now makes a fifth appearance with his second classic quintet. And his sixth appearance is over the page. Bear with me, you'll be convinced!

ESP: Miles Davis's second classic quintet had it in abundance.

After *Kind of Blue* and *Sketches of Spain* in 1959–60, Miles was at a slightly low ebb. John Coltrane had gone off to form his own quartet, and Miles tried various saxophonists who, good in their own right, never quite fit in. He was also churning out the same limited repertoire, mixing old standards—*My Funny Valentine, Stella by Starlight*—and newer compositions—*All Blues, So What*—but this was old music. Miles needed a change.

" ☆ "

Cover art

In the early 1960s Miles noted that he had never seen a black woman on a record cover unless she was the artist. *ESP* therefore featured his wife Frances Taylor, but by 1967 she had been replaced by actress Cicely Tyson, who appears on the front cover of *Sorcerer*. A year later, Miles had married Betty Mabry, who graces *Filles de Kilimanjaro*.

Miles Davis, setting the pace once again.

1967 Francis Chichester completes his solo around-the-world voyage in the *Gypsy Moth IV*. The journey lasts 119 days and is the longest non-stop voyage ever made in a small sailing ship.

1968 At the Olympic Games in Mexico, Dick Fosbury wins a gold medal with his unique "Fosbury Flop."

1968 Robert Redford opens Sundance, an ecological ski resort.

The quintet

The phenomenal Tony Williams (1945–97) was an orchestral drummer, providing a fluid, ambiguous rhythmic pulse that allowed the improvisers great freedom. Where a soloist went, he followed, echoing the melodic patterns. Anchoring the rhythm section were Herbie Hancock (b.1940) on piano and Ron Carter (b.1937) on bass. Ideas came from saxophonist Wayne Shorter (b.1933), like Hancock a mainstay of Blue Note records. Shorter's oblique, asymmetrical phrasing was matched by an understated, urbane melancholy. It was a winning combination.

Left to right, Herbie Hancock, Miles Davis, Ron Carter, Wayne Shorter, with Tony Williams in the background.

It came in 1964 when the final ingredient of a new quintet—saxophonist Wayne Shorter—joined from Art Blakey's Jazz Messengers. The new quintet were all younger than Miles—drummer Tony Williams was only 17 when he joined in 1963—and they revived both him and his music. With Shorter and pianist Herbie Hancock supplying most of the compositions, the group developed a way of playing known as "time—no changes." While the pulse remained regular, and was often implied rather than stated, there was no harmonic sequence based on chord changes, and no fixed length for solos. Instead, the soloist developed the opening melodic fragment in whatever way he liked, piano and bass following his lead. Drummer Williams kept up a dialogue with the rest of the band. Miles now played longer lines and departed from the middle register more often. All this resulted in ethereal, almost abstract pieces, often modal, that were as far away from the standard bop repertoire as possible. It was also unique—no other group sounded like this. Miles was back on top.

Six studio albums, as well as one epic live session, came out of this stellar quintet, which set new standards of jazz performance. But listen closely to *Miles in the Sky*, their penultimate album, recorded in 1968. On *Stuff*, Hancock plays electric piano and Ron Carter electric bass. On *Paraphernalia*, George Benson joins in on electric guitar. It was official—Miles was going electric.

ALL THAT JAZZ

MILES DAVIS—*ESP, Miles Smiles, Sorcerer, Nefertiti, Miles in the Sky, Filles de Kilimanjaro*: the classic quintet albums; *Miles Davis Quintet 1965–68* (6 CDs): complete and collected studio sessions; *The Complete Live at the Plugged Nickel* (7 CDs): live in Chicago, December 1965 (all Columbia).
HERBIE HANCOCK—*Takin' Off, Maiden Voyage, Empyrean Isles, Speak Like a Child* (all Blue Note).
WAYNE SHORTER—*Night Dreamer, Juju, Speak No Evil, Adam's Apple* (all Blue Note)

1969 Neil Armstrong is the first man to walk on the moon.

1970 The World Trade Center in New York becomes the world's tallest building.

1972 Elton John's hit single *Rocket Man* zooms up the charts.

1969~1975

Miles in the Sky
Electric Miles Davis

Miles's album covers, like his music, reflected his tilt at the rock market.

Last shout for Miles! And some shout, for this is where jazz meets rock in a big way. The meeting, predictably enough, was orchestrated by Miles, and again, predictably enough, was completely unpredictable in its outcome, for in anyone else's hands the collision of jazz and rock would have been loud and clamorous. With Miles the collision was initially quiet. In a Silent Way *changed the face of jazz forever, and many would say that jazz has never recovered since.*

Visitors to Miles during 1968 were amazed to find him listening to soul singers such as James Brown and Aretha Franklin and rock stars such as the Fifth Dimension and the Byrds. Some racial and stylistic mix there, but what united them was the mass popularity of rock music; ever since the Beatles, jazz was a minority music. Miles wanted that popularity, and moved to embrace it. Out went acoustic instruments, in came electric guitars, keyboards, and basses. Percussionists were brought in to beef up the rhythm section, and later sitars and flutes added the then de rigueur sound of India. Out went shortish tracks, in came long, continuous improvisations. Previously Miles had

Electric Miles: mass popularity, but a gradual withdrawal behind those shades was matched by the gradual withdrawal of his audience.

1973 In the Netherlands, driving on Sundays is banned in an attempt to preserve gasoline supplies.

1974 Uri Geller hits the headlines with his extraordinary ability to bend spoons and mend watches.

1975 The film *Star Wars* finally gets the go-ahead from 20th Century-Fox's board of directors.

recorded sparsely; now he couldn't be kept out of the studio, working endlessly with producer Teo Macero to edit and splice the raw music into the finished product.

In a Silent Way, recorded in 1969, is sublime: two electric pianos and an electric organ shimmering alongside John McLaughlin's chiming electric guitar over a light-touch metronomic pulse from Tony Williams. Wayne Shorter slides over the top with a drop-dead gorgeous soprano sax line, matched only by an extraordinarily graceful Miles. Far more gentle than its predecessors, far quieter than its successors, *In a Silent Way* was guaranteed to shock. But not half as much as *Bitches Brew*, released the following year. Using anything up to 13 musicians, the music is deeper, darker, and as abstract as anything Miles had ever played before. A powerful rock beat drives all before it, and drove it onto the album charts. It was Miles's biggest selling record to date, and it got him dates in rock venues across the country. But here something odd happened. Rock music

Miles the rock star: keyboards, festivals, huge amplification, media attention, the lot.

Who's Jack Johnson?
You shouldn't have to ask, but since you have, Jack Johnson (1878–1946) was the first black heavyweight champion of the world, holding the title from 1908 to 1915; he later owned Harlem's Cotton Club. Miles was a boxing fanatic and recorded the soundtrack for a documentary about his hero. The music is truly grand, with John McLaughlin playing his socks off. This is the nearest Miles came to straightahead rock, and it is unequivocally superb.

was all about songs and instrumental hook lines, and live rock music was big-hearted and welcoming to its audience. But what Miles was playing was claustrophobic and schizophrenic, a music that seesawed between strong rhythmic grooves and abstract interplay. By the time he recorded *Agharta* and *Pangaea*—both live sets from Japan in 1975—Miles was lost in a dense electronic rain forest, and he had lost his audience, too. So Miles retired, taking a sabbatical that lasted for six years.

1972 Bob Marley is signed to Island records and becomes the first reggae star to break into the mainstream music scene.

1973 The Getty family agrees to pay a $1 million ransom for their kidnapped son Paul, after they receive his ear in the mail.

1982 The late Elvis Presley's sumptuous home Graceland opens to the public.

1969~present

Jazz + Rock = Fusion

Williams, McLaughlin, Shorter, Corea, Hancock

Look closely at the names on this page. Every one of them played with Miles Davis. And most of their records are on Columbia, Miles's label, which hit gold with jazz-rock and mined it for all it was worth. For where Miles went, his musicians followed, and often with more success. Perversely, their vast popularity needled Miles, for what he had sown and failed to reap, his disciples profited by immensely.

Birds of Fire, fusion from the Mahavishnu Orchestra led by John McLaughlin.

Tony WILLIAMS (1945–97) was first in on the act, setting up the loud, rugged, blues-tinged trio Lifetime with *Larry YOUNG* (1940–78)—"the John Coltrane of the organ"—and British-born guitarist *John McLAUGHLIN* (b.1942) to record *Emergency!* in May 1969, some three months before the *Bitches Brew* sessions. Lifetime was too raw, too intense for most people, nearer the blues powerhouse of Cream or the Jimi Hendrix Experience than a traditional jazz trio, but it opened the door. And through that door went John McLaughlin, who on leaving

John McLaughlin, an effortless virtuoso, all the way from Yorkshire.

1986 Nicotine chewing gum is introduced for the first time.

1993 Vikram Seth's *A Suitable Boy* (1000 pages) becomes the longest novel to be published in English in 245 years.

1996 The first McDonald's opens in India. Pride of place on the beef-free menu is given to the mutton-only Maharajah Mac.

Future Shock by Herbie Hancock. In his hands the future was adventurous, but the future of jazz was not to be found in funk.

HERBIE HANCOCK

As jazz-rock flourished during the 1970s, one man initially floundered: *Herbie HANCOCK* (b.1940). His first band, Mwandishi, toured the States in 1972 with a synthesizer and struggled to cope with the new electronic technology—synthesizers couldn't be preprogrammed in those days, which made them all but useless on stage. The music was complex and failed to pay its way, so in 1973, with a new band, Hancock recorded the ebullient, funky *Headhunters*, the biggest and fastest-selling jazz album of all time. It was the album that gave jazz-rock a good name, and spawned a million prodigies with Afro haircuts and Spandex suits. They in turn reduced much of jazz-rock to jazz-funk and ultimately jazz-lite. It pleased the customers, but was it jazz?

Lifetime put together the Mahavishnu Orchestra in 1971. With mountains of amplifiers and a prodigious jazz guitar technique out of Hendrix and R&B, McLaughlin combined Indian lyricism with hard rock to noisy effect. The contrast with Miles was huge—where *Bitches Brew* and its successors were often turgid and congested, McLaughlin's music was clean and in its way simple, with predetermined unison riffs, soloists trading two- and four-bar statements, and lots of well-rehearsed counterpoint played over whirlwind drumming. McLaughlin learned quickly what Miles failed to realize—that new technology meant new instrumental techniques, with the complexities of jazz too subtle for this new style.

Not all the Miles men went for volume. *Wayne SHORTER* (b.1933) teamed up with organist *Joe ZAWINUL* (b.1932) in 1971 to form Weather Report, one of the great jazz ensembles until its demise in 1986. Named by Shorter because its music changed "from day to day like the weather," Weather Report was subtle, melodic, and infinitely varied. Less varied was Return to Forever, a Latin-tinged group formed by *Chick COREA* (b.1941) in 1972.

Fusion, jazz-rock, and funk

Time for terms, and none are more confusing or interchangeable than these three. Fusion is the merger of two or more different types of music. In the 1960s, British free-jazz pioneer Joe Harriott ran a group called Indo-Jazz Fusions, which mixed a jazz sextet with an Indian classical quartet to great effect. But the fusion most talked about is that of jazz and rock, which dominated jazz in the 1970s. Jazz-rock combined the improvisational techniques of modern jazz with the instrumentation and rhythmic approach of rock. Other musical styles were pulled into this fusion—John McLaughlin brought in Indian music with the Mahavishnu Orchestra, while Chick Corea added Latin and classical music. Much of jazz-rock is also funky, using the complex, syncopated rhythms of 1960s soul music, popularized by James Brown and later Sly Stone, and is best termed jazz-funk; but funk music has a distinct lineage and life of its own.

1972 Pope Paul VI pays the first papal visit to Britain in 450 years.

1980 Irish rock band U2 releases its first album, *Boy*.

1982 The surgical technique of liposuction is used to remove excess fat from the body.

1966~present

Improv

European Free Improvisation

Trevor Watts' *Moiré Music*: seamless textures from a European loom.

One of the great strengths of jazz music in the past thirty years or so has been the wealth of improvised music produced away from the big concert halls and clubs and unrecorded by the major labels. Some has surfaced and made it big time, but most has remained of minor interest, despite the musicianship of those involved. And none has remained more in the shadows than the array of music sheltering under the label of European improvised music, or improv.

Circular breathing

A technique used by some reed players, notably British improvising saxophonist Evan Parker (b.1944), circular breathing involves inhaling through the nose while the cheeks push the air out into the instrument. This results in a single column of air that allows the musician to play continuous lines, without breathing spaces. It might sound like a party trick, but some music demands it!

We need some signposts here, for improv is not really free jazz. Whatever it might sound like to you, free jazz is still jazz, with at least some elements linking in with the mainstream of jazz development. But improv is what trumpeter Leo Smith once described as the individual's "ability to instantaneously organize sound, silence

Evan Parker, a stalwart of European free jazz.

and rhythm with the whole of his or her creative intelligence." More succinctly, it is "the exploration of occasion," which is likely to be a small club or room where like-minded performers play to an audience of aficionados. The music might reflect the musical interests of those involved—jazz, folk, electronic, classical, or the avant-garde, *musique concrète* or whatever—or might

1985 Bulgarian-born American artist Christo wraps Paris's Pont Neuf in fabric.

1988 President Ronald Reagan is reported to consult an astrologer before every important event.

1997 The Internet system crashes for the first time, causing Web-chaos.

Derek Bailey: uncompromising, individual, and utterly unique.

well transcend them in pursuit of a true and instantaneous improvisation, untainted by past associations.

If American improv has stuck close to free jazz and tended to the individualistic —soloists emerging from the ensemble— the European variant has been more collective, concerned with processes rather than personal expression. AMM (an acronym which has remained forever secret) incorporated found sounds from transistor radios and elsewhere, and often performed in the dark to emphasize the selfless nature of their approach. Likewise the Spontaneous Music Ensemble, which has pursued collectively generated music with no preconceived structures of any sort. A mainstay of European improv has been guitarist *Derek BAILEY* (b.1930), a solo and duo performer of infinite variety who, through his loose collective Company, has involved musicians from a wide variety of backgrounds in pursuit of the elusive improvisational spark.

With so little space and so many names, this is but a glimpse into a mind-set all of its own. It might be a case of all the usual suspects in lots of unusual combinations, but for sheer vitality and uncommerciality, improv is its own howling gale of musical invention.

ALL THAT JAZZ

AMM—*AMMMUSIC 1966* (Matchless).
DEREK BAILEY—*Solo Guitar* (Incus, 2 volumes).
COMPANY—*Company 6 & 7* (Incus).
SPONTANEOUS MUSIC ENSEMBLE—*Karyobin* (Chronoscope).
TREVOR WATTS' MOIRÉ MUSIC—*With One Voice* (Arc, LP only)—a leading free-jazzer in approachable form.

Joe Harriott

In all the arguments about free jazz and who invented it, one name keeps coming up. Jamaican-born Joe Harriott (1928–73) moved to Britain in 1951 and became a fine bop alto saxophonist. In 1959 he conceived of a music, written and improvised, without set harmonic or rhythmic structures. Unlike Coleman's experiments in the U.S., which while harmonically abstract were still jazz-based, Harriott's music was totally abstract, with no regular rhythm, jagged dissonances, free improvisation, periods of silence, and elements of Afro-Caribbean music all fused together. Sadly, it was no contest, and in comparison with Coleman, his achievements went all but unrecognized. But his legacy lives on in countless improv sessions.

1973 The mountain bike is invented by members of the Marin County Canyon cycling club in California.

1983 Madonna, described by some as having a voice like "Minnie Mouse on helium," releases her first album, *Madonna*.

1986 British health minister Edwina Currie blames poor health in the north of Britain on "ignorance."

1966~present

Escalators over Hills

Carla Bley, Charlie Haden, George Russell

Gathering of the clans: Charlie Haden's *Liberation Music Orchestra*.

Meanwhile, back in the Jurassic Big Band Park, the rush of experimentation that hit jazz in the 1960s spawned a new generation of big bands that came to life at the end of the decade. Do we want to give them a label? "Art bands" would do, although that implies a seriousness and pretentiousness above and beyond the call of duty. In most cases, serious was not a word in their vocabulary: anarchic, exhilarating, and extraordinary better describe the creative outpourings from these big ensembles.

In at the October Revolution was *Carla Bley* (b.1938), a California-born pianist and composer who, with her then partner Mike Mantler, founded the Jazz Composer's Orchestra in 1965. Out of this pool of New York's finest came some memorable large-scale jazz works, notably *Liberation Music Orchestra* by Ornette Coleman's bass player *Charlie Haden* (b.1937), a collection inspired by the Spanish Civil War, including *We Shall Overcome* and Haden's own *Song for Che*. Bley herself labored for three years on a two-hour jazz opera *Escalator over the Hill*, released in 1971 and mysteriously subtitled "A Chronotransduction," which covered all the bases from big band to prototype world music. In Europe, the vast

pool of jazz, free and improvising musicians coalesced around several projects, most adventurously the 50-piece Centipede (50 people, two legs each, equals...) and the later 22-piece Ark (two by two)—both sadly absent from the record catalog—formed by the British

George Russell, always happy to show the way.

1987 Hungarian-born Italian porn star Illana Staller is elected to the Italian parliament.

1988 Computer systems all over the world fail due to hacker-implanted viruses.

1996 Mad Cow Disease alarms Britain and the worldwide export of British beef and beef products is banned by the European Commission.

pianist *Keith TIPPETT* (b.1947); the various bands of British composer *Mike WESTBROOK* (b.1936); the Globe Unity Orchestra, formed by German pianist *Alexander von SCHLIPPENBACH* (b.1938) in 1966; the London Jazz Composers Orchestra of bass player *Barry GUY* (b.1947), formed in 1970; the Kollektief of Dutchman *Willem BREUKER* (b.1944), established in 1974; and the Vienna Art Orchestra of Swiss-born *Mathias RÜEGG* (b.1952), established in 1977.

Despite their different nationalities, these big bands had much in common. The international language of jazz jostled for space

Live and leggy and totally anarchic: Carla Bley.

with the free improvising tradition of European jazz, inspired by all those South Africans we saw head into exile in the 1960s, but theater and performance art also contributed much to their presentation. Revolutionary or anarchic politics lay behind some of the music, overt in the case of Haden, translated through Brecht/Eisler/Weill in the cases of Bley and Breuker, while personnel moved with ease from one to the other. Economically, these bands were anachronisms, but musically their force and vitality did much to reinvigorate jazz in the 1970s. And of course it goes without saying they were quite fabulous to watch live, a joint in one hand, a revolutionary tract or drink in the other (delete one or all as personally appropriate). When did you last have such fun at a jazz concert—or any concert, for that matter?

ALL THAT JAZZ

CARLA BLEY—*Escalator over the Hill* (JCOA, 2 CDs); *Tropic Appetites, The Very Big Carla Bley Band* (both Watt).
WILLEM BREUKER—*The Parrot* (BVHAAST).
GLOBE UNITY ORCHESTRA—*20th Anniversary* (FMP).
CHARLIE HADEN—*Liberation Music Orchestra* (Impulse), *The Ballad of the Fallen* (ECM).
LONDON JAZZ COMPOSERS ORCHESTRA—*Ode, Harmos, Theoria, Portraits* (2 CDs) (all Intakt).
GEORGE RUSSELL—*The Essence of George Russell, New York Big Band* (both Soul Note).
VIENNA ART ORCHESTRA—*The Minimalism of Eric Satie* (hat ART).
MIKE WESTBROOK—*The Cortège* (Enja, 2 CDs); *Marching Song* (Deram, 2 CDs).

George Russell

The unlikely figure of George Russell (b.1923), once a drummer with the Benny Carter Orchestra and the composer of *Cubana Be, Cubana Bop* for Dizzy Gillespie in the 1940s, has provided jazz with its single most important theoretical treatise: *The Lydian Chromatic Concept of Tonal Organization*. Written in the early 1950s, it was the source of the modal innovations pioneered by Miles Davis, and assimilated modal writing with the extreme chromaticism of contemporary music, showing arrangers and improvisers how to reconcile formal scoring with the freedom of improvisation. Russell worked from jazz practice rather than principle, and turned his theories into very fine big band practice. Students of jazz need to study his book, listeners can rest assured that theory does not get in the way of some energizing big band music.

1973 Country and Western singer Tammy Wynette gets to number one in the American charts with her hit song *Stand by Your Man*.

1974 The craze for "streaking" hits Britain and the U.S.

1977 The Pompidou Centre opens in Paris.

1971~present
In Concert, Alone
Keith Jarrett

Keith JARRETT (b.1945)—where do we start with you? With at least five different Jarretts in operation at any time, and a record label apparently willing to release an annual boxed set of "Jarrett Plays Three Blind Mice," separating the wood from the trees is a problem here. So let's start on November 10, 1971.

Jarrett and the groups

Jarrett was plucked by Miles Davis to play electric organ and piano in 1970–71, but turned his back on fusion and went solo and acoustic in 1972. In his early years, Jarrett ran two overlapping groups—an American quartet and a European quartet. The American quartet was more experimental but more erratic, while the European quartet was marked by Jarrett's close relationship with saxophonist Jan Garbarek, continued on numerous duo and other albums.

Keith Jarrett alone at the piano—where else?—with only his verbal exclamations and interjections for company. Heroic in every sense.

O n that day, Jarrett recorded a totally improvised solo piano album for ECM, a new European label. *Facing You* became a great success, launching the enduring Jarrett–ECM partnership, and encouraged him to undertake a solo tour around Europe in 1973 playing nothing but improvised music. Recordings of two concerts—Lausanne and Bremen—were released on a triple-album set that sold 350,000 copies over

Solo improvisation

Jarrett has taken solo piano improvisation to unprecedented heights. Before a solo concert, he tries to clear his mind of all preconceived ideas and then lets his creativity take control. His concerts are totally improvised stream-of-consciousness creations: everything started from scratch. To participate in one of these concerts is to witness an artist wrestling with himself to come up with ideas, sometimes marking time before inspiration leads him in a new direction. Inevitably, he falls back on certain trademark phrases, for Jarrett keeps well within the melodic and harmonic mainstream of jazz, but in every sense they are heroic performances that stand or fall on the imagination of the performer on the night.

the next decade, an unheard-of success for "difficult" music. By now, Jarrett was in full flow: the recording of a concert in Köln has become one of the best-selling jazz albums of all time (two million copies plus)

1982 Michael Fagan breaks into Buckingham Palace, steals a bottle of wine, sits on the Queen's bed, and asks for a cigarette.

1991 Carl Lewis sets a world record for the 100-meter sprint of 9.85 seconds.

1997 Comet Hale-Bopp, independently discovered in 1995 by two amateur astrologers, Alan Hale in New Mexico and Thomas Bopp in Arizona, makes its closest approach to Earth on March 23.

and has probably kept ECM in the black ever since, while the 10-LP (6-CD) *Sun Bear* set recorded in Japan in 1976 plunged his audience heavily into debt for the rest of the decade. Five more solo piano albums have subsequently appeared.

To add to this substantial achievement, Jarrett has revisited the American popular songbook in the company of bassist *Gary Peacock* (b.1935) and drummer *Jack DeJohnette* (b.1942). To date, ten sets of songs have appeared, as well as two sets— *Changes* and *Changeless*—of the trio in improvising mode.

To the solo Jarrett and the standards Jarrett must be added the group Jarrett, the classical Jarrett—playing Shostakovich, Bach, and his own orchestral compositions— and the all-purpose Jarrett

Another string to his bow, for Jarrett is also a fine classical composer.

At the Deer Head Inn

It is the dream of every overblown rock star to return to their roots and play small clubs again. Endearingly, Jarrett did just that in September 1992, playing a trio set to relaunch the Deer Head Inn jazz club in his birthplace of Allentown, Pennsylvania, scene of his first jazz gig in 1961.

playing everything from solo pipe organ and clavichord to overdubbed ethnic instruments, either by himself or with like-minded chums. All on ECM, of course ("All that Jazz" is merely a cursory glance at his total output). Some would say that it is impossible to have too much of a good thing. Others would argue that one role for a record company is to tell an artist to take a long vacation. But for his almost single-handed mission to keep jazz acoustic in the face of fusion, and for his superb standards trio—on a good day the equal of Bill Evans—Jarrett deserves all the applause he gets. There might be an inferior album every so often, but there are many people who own only one jazz record, and they like *The Köln Concert* real fine. They aren't wrong; the rest of us must select with care

ALL THAT JAZZ

SOLO STUDIO PIANO: *Facing You*.
SOLO LIVE PIANO: *Solo Concerts Bremen/ Lausanne* (2 CDs), *The Köln Concert, Sun Bear Concerts* (6 CDs), *Concerts* (Bregenz), *Vienna Concert, La Scala*.
STANDARDS TRIO: *Standards Vol. 1, Vol. 2, Changes, Standards Live, Still Live* (2 CDs), *Changeless, Bye Bye Blackbird, At the Blue Note* (6 CDs), *Tokyo '96*.
WITH PEACOCK AND PAUL MOTIAN: *At the Deer Head Inn*.
AMERICAN QUARTET: *Mysteries: The Impulse! Years 1975–76* (Impulse, 4 CDs)
EUROPEAN QUARTET: *Belonging, My Song, Personal Mountains*.

1972 The first Polaroid SX-70 instant cameras go on sale.

1983 Harold Washington becomes the first black mayor of Chicago.

1984 Jane Torvill and Christopher Dean are given top marks for their performance to Ravel's *Bolero* at the Winter Olympics.

1969~present
Nordic Freeze
ECM Records

In a book dedicated to product—music—it seems out of place to have an entire entry dedicated to process—a record label. What counts, surely, is the music itself, not the label on which it appears? But jazz labels have their own identities, often based on the musical interests of their founders or producers, and listeners will recognize and applaud the quality of a hard bop album from, say, Blue Note, as they will a free music album from Impulse. And no label has a stronger identity than ECM—Editions of Contemporary Music— established in Cologne in 1969 by bassist Manfred Eicher.

Withholding Pattern by John Surman, a typically cool title and image from ECM.

Like Blue Note, ECM has a strong visual identity—muted colors, clever typography and graphics, and moody black-and-white photographs of empty landscapes adorn their covers—but what most distinguishes the label is the quality of its recordings. A clean, well-defined, sometimes sterile sound with immaculate attention to detail has led to accusations that ECM is cold-blooded and melancholic. Fair enough criticism, for few other labels would issue solo cello or bandoneon albums (deeply tearful!). But while there is a certain bleakness to many of its recordings, ECM has also been home to some of the best and most lively Art Ensemble sets, as well as bringing us the double glories of Jan Garbarek and John Surman.

Norwegian saxophonist Jan Garbarek, ECM star and crossover specialist.

Norwegian saxophonist *Jan GARBAREK* (b.1947) led on an early ECM album—*Afric Pepperbird*—and has developed his keening saxophone sound away from early free-jazz influences toward a folk-oriented style that is utterly distinctive. One of his bestselling albums is not even jazz—*Officium* pairs him with the Hilliard vocal ensemble in a set of medieval church music. English-born saxophonist *John SURMAN* (b.1944) has followed a similar trajectory: his latest album, *Proverbs and Songs*, finds him in England's Salisbury Cathedral with organ and chorus, and was even nominated for the prestigious Mercury Prize for best British album of 1998, alongside The Verve and Robbie Williams! More representative are his solo albums, where he overdubs soprano and baritone saxophones, bass clarinet, and synthesizers in a gorgeously evocative mix of English folk and electronics.

I've picked two saxophonists, but I could equally have picked a pair of trumpeters or bass players or pianists or guitarists to illustrate the range of ECM music. Innovative in their embrace of Third World musics, and indulgent enough to their artists in releasing the sometimes unreleasable, ECM has defined and delineated a style of jazz that is quite unlike any other. Ikea music to some, a way of life to others. Ignore it at your (discriminating) peril.

HIP CATS

Finnish drummer and composer **Edward Vesala** *(b.1945) played with Garbarek in the early 1970s. A Vesala album sounds like nothing else in jazz—heavily composed ensemble pieces using up to eleven musicians playing a mix of folk and popular music. Dark moods alternate with lighter arrangements; perversely, the latter are the more sinister, the former being kept for more tongue-in-cheek stuff. His five albums for ECM, recorded between 1974 and 1994, give the lie to those who criticize ECM for being too cautious, for these sets are cutting-edge stuff.*

ALL THAT JAZZ

JAN GARBAREK—*Afric Pepperbird; Dis:* Garbarek with brass sextet in glorious form; *Twelve Moons; Officium; Ragas And Sagas:* Jan meets Sufi singers and musicians from Pakistan.
DAVE HOLLAND—*Life Cycle:* solo cello.
Dino Saluzzi—*Andina; Once upon a Time—Far Away in the South:* that tear-jerking bandoneon player solo and in a quartet!
JOHN SURMAN—*Upon Reflection, Withholding Pattern, Road to St. Ives* (all solo); *Proverbs and Songs.*
Edward Vesala—*Nan Madol, Lumi, Ode to the Death of Jazz, Invisible Storm, Nordic Gallery.*

Jan Garbarek Group, with Eberhard Weber, Rainer Bruninghaus, and Marilyn Mazur.

1976 America celebrates 200 years of independence with its bicentennial 4th of July festivities.

1979 The Sony Walkman makes its first appearance.

1982 Actor Dustin Hoffman gives one of cinema's best drag performances in the film *Tootsie*.

1974~present

Six Strings, Two Heads

Pat Metheny

There are two Pat Methenys—the jazz-lite guitarist who, rock-starlike, fills stadiums with his easy-listening tunes, and the cutting-edge guitarist whose work is as robust and vigorous as any of the celebrated musicians he works with. Versatile or schizophrenic? Or are we just talking here about different degrees of success—commercial, critical, personal—attained by a musician to whom boundaries are there to be trashed?

American Garage, from an on-the-road specialist.

Missouri-born *Pat Metheny* (b.1954) was teaching at the prestigious Berklee College of Music in Boston while he was still a teenager, before playing in vibraphonist Gary Burton's quintet from 1974 to 1976. Those clever people at ECM picked him up and promoted him in the mid-1970s as a cool, limpid guitarist, in retrospect just the right antidote to the overblown jazz-rockers of the 1970s. With keyboard player *Lyle Mays* (b.1953) on board from his second album, *Watercolors*, Metheny has been both prolific and popular. His tone is clean and open, with a fine line in hummable tunes drawn from jazz, rock, and country music, and long, loping, highly melodic solos. He uses enough electronics to enhance his sound, but remains at heart a

Pat Metheny: the user-friendly face of jazz.

" ☆ "

Where in the world?

Unlikely collaboration of the year came in 1985, when the Pat Metheny Group backed rock singer David Bowie on *This Is Not America*, the theme tune for John Schlesinger's film *The Falcon and the Snowman*, for which Metheny also wrote the soundtrack. The single did well in both British and American singles charts, but it sure sounded like America to us.

1987 Britain is devastated by hurricanes only hours after an official forecast of calm weather.

1994 Investigations begin into the 'Whitewater' affair between the Clintons and Arkansas banker James McDougal.

1997 "Girl power" Spice Girls become the first pop band to have a U.K. number-one hit with each of their first four singles and are deemed the most successful all-girl lineup ever.

traditional jazz guitarist keeping select company. The title track of 1981's *As Falls Wichita, So Falls Wichita Falls*, with its playground noises, swirling synths, and Brazilian rhythms from percussion maestro *Nana VASCONCELOS* (b.1944), is particularly effective and atmospheric.

Rejoicing, recorded in 1983, showed that there was more to Metheny than had been suspected. With Ornette Coleman alumni Charlie Haden on bass and Billy Higgins on drums, Metheny recorded an album of Coleman and Haden tunes, with a brace of his own songs which, while lilting and rather respectful, showed some steel in his soul. *Song X*, his first for the new Geffen label, made the break in a big way. Coleman himself and drummer son Denardo, as well as Haden and drummer Jack DeJohnette, powered their way through a set of Coleman originals, with few hostages to the expectations of a typical Metheny audience. Even more extreme was *Zero Tolerance for Silence*, a riot of electronic solo guitar in complete contrast to the jazz-lite, lite-rock feel of his latest albums. *Song X* is courageous, *Zero Tolerance* close to self-indulgent, but full marks to Metheny for having the courage of his convictions and playing on his terms. But can you bear the noise?

Modern jazz guitar

By the 1970s there were two distinct strands of guitar performance in jazz. One, the amplified, acoustic, mild-mannered approach that owed everything to Wes Montgomery (1925–68), the other, electric and blues-powered, that traced its lineage back through Jimi Hendrix (1942–70) to Muddy Waters (1915–83) and the first electric blues guitarists. Metheny was influenced by Montgomery, whose cleanly articulated lines, unflappable poise, and easy swing made everything seem effortless. Jim Hall (b.1930) and Joe Pass (1929–84), the guitarist of choice for Oscar Peterson and Ella Fitzgerald, are in the same bag, as is George Benson (b.1943), whose fluent ease brought him huge commercial success playing jazz-funk after his stint with Miles Davis in the late 1960s. Apart from Metheny, ECM has nurtured a number of basically acoustic guitarists, notably John Abercrombie (b.1944), Egberto Gismonti (b.1947), and Ralph Towner (b.1940), all multi-instrumentalists whose use of electronics and interest in Third World music break down the boundaries of the jazz tradition.

Wes Montgomery, unflappable guitar poise.

1979 The satirical film *Monty Python's Life of Brian* is greeted with ecclesiastical outrage.

1980 In Britain the Rubik's cube is voted "Toy of the Year."

1982 Rap makes a breakthrough into mainstream pop with the hit *The Message* by Grandmaster Flash and the Furious Five.

1975~present

Dancing in Your Head
Ornette Coleman

Joujouka in Morocco.

For the third time in his career, Ornette Coleman set critical hackles rising. Not content with turning jazz upside down in 1959, and then upsetting the purists with his self-taught violin and trumpet playing in 1965, Ornette returned in 1975 with an electric band playing jazz-funk. The date is important, for this was the year Miles admitted defeat and went into semiretirement for six years. But Ornette was more astute, and his band—Prime Time— much more approachable than Miles's electronic jungle troops.

Ornette has always been concerned with the communication and reception of his music, and in Prime Time he found the perfect vehicle to broadcast more widely. Joined on stage by pairs of electric guitars, basses, and drums setting up elaborate dialogues with each other, Coleman continued to play acoustic alto, amplified to make himself audible, although his style remained unchanged. Great was the noise, but the heart was uplifted, for Prime Time delivered a truly joyous sound. Elements of rock, Berber folk— Coleman visited the Moroccan village of Joujouka in 1973 and recorded with its legendary Master Musicians—free jazz

James "Blood" Ulmer, Coleman collaborator and co-visionary.

Harmolodic disciples

The harmolodic messiah has two main disciples: drummer Ronald Shannon Jackson (b.1940) and guitarist James "Blood" Ulmer (b.1942). Jackson played on *Dancing in Your Head* before recording one of the most important albums of the 1980s, *Decode Yourself*, as yet unavailable on CD. A propulsive drummer, he has done much to popularize harmolodics among black rock musicians. James "Blood" Ulmer has the distinction of playing harmolodics almost before Ornette, his landmark *Tales of Captain Black* recorded with the maestro in 1978. *Are You Glad to Be in America?*, a rough, raw slab of harmolodic blues, brought Ulmer huge critical attention in 1980 for its punkish leanings, and he has since led two acclaimed but differing bands—the Music Revelation Ensemble with saxophonist David Murray (b.1955), of whom more later, and Phalanx with saxophonist George Adams (1940–92). *Odyssey* from 1983 represents a change of scene, Ulmer in almost folkish form with stripped-down violin and drums, but recent albums have been almost boorish as Ulmer searches for a new harmolodic language closer to R&B.

1988 Britain's Queen Elizabeth II and the Duke of Edinburgh are booed on their tour of Australia.

1993 The 150th Grand National horse race is abandoned after two false starts; bookies are forced to return around £60 million to bettors.

1995 The widely publicized O.J. Simpson saga ends as the jury finds him not guilty of the murder of his former wife Nicole Brown Simpson and her friend Ronald Goldman.

and jazz-rock coalesce in this music, but don't be deterred, for the music is its own amalgam and there is nothing daunting here. Most approachable is *Virgin Beauty*, released in 1988, on which the Grateful Dead guitarist Jerry Garcia guested on three tracks. Coleman had witnessed a Grateful Dead concert and was amazed at the devotion of the assembled Deadheads. Garcia brought kudos to Coleman, but in reality Coleman already had his own legions and Garcia's contribution was slight. Of historic interest is *In All Languages*, released in 1987 to celebrate "30 Years of Harmolodic Music." We're glad Coleman reminded us, since no one would have thought to have baked a cake, but he celebrated in style, recording an acoustic side to the then-double album

Harmolodics

Another label, and this one's a puzzle. Coleman claims he has played harmolodics since his ground-breaking albums of the late 1950s, but few of his musicians had ever heard of it. The word itself combines harmony, movement (rhythm), and melody, indicating the equality both between the different elements of the music and between the different musicians—in other words, the basic principle of instrumental democracy already established in free jazz. To hear it in operation is to hear a single melodic or thematic line played simultaneously in different tones and pitches by different musicians, resulting in a gloriously jangling romp. The theory is complex, the sound is not.

Prime time

"The name was given because every rehearsal was done in such a will-it-be or not-be manner (because of the difficulty of scheduling everybody for rehearsals). When it did happen it was Prime Time." So said Ornette in the cover notes to *Body Meta*.

At Newport in 1977, with Don Cherry and Dewey Redman.

with his old quartet of Charlie Haden, Don Cherry, and Billy Higgins, and an electric side with his six-piece Prime Time. Compare and contrast, since many of the pieces overlap. Likewise the two volumes of *Sound Museum—Hidden Man* and *Three Women*—where the quartet, now including pianist *Geri ALLEN* (b.1957), plays the same pieces in two different ways. Darker and more haunting than some recent Prime Time music, *Sound Museum* curates a musician in his prime.

ALL THAT JAZZ

ORNETTE COLEMAN—*Dancing in Your Head* (A&M); *Virgin Beauty* (Columbia); *Body Meta*, *In All Languages*, *Tone Dialing*, *Sound Museum* (two volumes) (all Verve).
RONALD SHANNON JACKSON—*Decode Yourself* (Island, LP only); *What Spirit Say* (DIW).
MUSIC REVELATION ENSEMBLE—*Electric Jazz* (DIW).
JAMES "BLOOD" ULMER—*Tales of Captain Black* (DIW); *Are You Glad to Be in America?* (Rough Trade, LP only); *Odyssey* (Columbia); *Original Phalanx* (DIW)

1976 Punk rock explodes onto the British pop scene, and the Sex Pistols hit the headlines for using bad language on television.

1984 A four-week-old baby is given a heart transplant from a baboon and survives 20 days.

1987 Soviet Yuri Romanenko returns to Earth after an 11-month stay in space.

1975~present

Out of the Lofts
Murray, Bang, and Zorn

Each decade of jazz has its distinct identity, despite their obvious overlaps, and the 1970s were no exception. The fires of the 1960s were burning out, and the next generation sought a way back from the extremes without selling out, reverting to stale tradition, or joining the fusion bandwagon. In New York, the availability of cheap(ish) lofts allowed young musicians space to practice and perform, making a name for themselves away from establishment clubs. Two figures stand out— although, as ever, a raft of names present themselves.

David Murray, one of the most important saxophonists since John Coltrane.

John Zorn

After the loft-dwellers of the 1970s came the postmodernists of the 1980s, all ironic statements and appropriation of a throwaway culture. John Zorn (b.1953) personifies this group; his presence is felt on a thousand albums. A fine alto saxophonist and improviser—*Spy vs. Spy* is his treatment of Ornette's finest—he is absorbed by the movies, reworking Ennio Morricone soundtracks on *The Big Gundown* and issuing a vast collection of self-composed soundtracks on his own Tzadik label. His work-rate is astounding, and it is hard to get a handle on this musician. But the *Masada* series suggests that at least one culture, his own, has some hold on him.

David MURRAY (b.1955) is a tenor saxophonist— he also plays soprano and bass clarinet—who has created a synthesis out of classic jazz and the experiments of Coltrane and Ayler. His playing is generous, expansive, and melodic, ranging from

barreling hard bop and swing to the endearingly romantic. To listen to Murray—which is easy, given that Black Saint and DIW have documented him in as fulsome a way as ECM has Jarrett—is to hear the whole history of jazz unfold in front of you. On *Real Deal* he pairs up with percussionist *Milford GRAVES* (b.1941) for a set of almost free improvisation; on *Body and Soul*, he pays homage to Coleman Hawkins and the tenor tradition. *Shakill's Warrior* sees him examining soul jazz in the company of *Don PULLEN* (1944–95) on Hammond organ, while *Ballads* and

1988 Picasso's painting *Acrobat and Young Harlequin* sells at auction for $38 million.

1996 A student claims a $70 million Harrier jet plane from PepsiCo as first prize in a Pepsi points competition. Pepsi countersues, claiming the prize offer was meant to be a joke.

1997 Dolly the sheep makes history by being the first successful clone.

John Zorn: unlistenable for many, but probably the biggest single inspiration for cutting-edge jazz today.

Spirituals are self-explanatory. His octet and big band are both Ellingtonian in scope; it's as if Murray is covering all the jazz bases in an attempt to simultaneously communicate, conserve, and develop the history of jazz all on his own.

Billy BANG (b. 1947)—who changed his name from Billy Walker because that was too anonymous—is one of the few musicians to develop a modern language for the violin. He plays it as if it were a percussion instrument, attacking every note with relish and delivering a mix of gypsy folk music, New Orleans swagger, and propulsive swing. Like Murray, Bang is a modernist, but he has enough traditional elements in his work to make him immediately

HIP CATS

Other names from the lofts to look out for include baritone saxophonist **Hamiet Bluiett** *(b. 1940) and alto saxophonists* **Julius Hemphill** *(1940–95), and* **Oliver Lake** *(b. 1944); these three together with David Murray made the World Saxophone Quartet. Also alto saxophonist* **Arthur Blythe** *(b. 1940), composer and bandleader* **Henry Threadgill** *(b. 1944), and trumpeter* **Olu Daru** *(b. 1941). Modernists all, they nevertheless remain in touch with the classic jazz tradition.*

The aptly named Billy Bang plays the violin with percussive flair.

accessible. *Live at Carlos 1* is a fine live album—don't ask for its successor, since Carlos 1 is the name of a New York club!—but for controled fire, his tributes to Coltrane on *Valve No. 10* are hard to beat.

1983 Vanessa Williams becomes the first black Miss America.

1984 Prince Charles attacks modern architecture in an address to the Royal Institute of British Architects.

1985 A new, sweeter Coca-Cola hits the market, but poor sales result in a return to the original recipe.

1980~present

In the Tradition

Wynton Marsalis

Hot House Flowers: Marsalis plus strings.

Backward we go, reversing out of the 1980s. For the biggest sensation to hit jazz for, well, a long time, is in the true sense of the word reactionary, reacting against the music of his time and returning jazz to a supposed golden age of "real" (i.e., acoustic) jazz, as heard from the 1920s to the Miles quintet of the 1960s. Wynton MARSALIS (b.1961) might play trumpet better than anyone since Miles, and has done more to popularize jazz with a new generation than the last great jazz popularizer—as well as winning every award going (the first to win simultaneous Grammys

Wynton Marsalis: the acceptable face of jazz?

in jazz and classical categories) and recording superb classical records for Deutsche Grammophon—but those excuses skirt around the fact that if Marsalis had his way, jazz would indeed go into reverse. But, and this is the biggest but of mitigation, Marsalis can play the rest of the jazz world off the stage. He is that good, and better.

Suitably, Wynton Marsalis was born into a jazz family in New Orleans and first came to everyone's notice as a member of the Jazz Messengers in 1980–82. His eponymous debut album used the famous rhythm section of Miles's 1960s quintet—Hancock, Carter, and Williams—on three tracks, and even covered *RJ*, Carter's composition which first appeared on *ESP*. Marsalis's interests range far and wide: on

ALL THAT JAZZ

GANELIN TRIO—*Catalogue: Live in East Germany* (Leo).
BRANFORD MARSALIS—*Scenes in the City, Buckshot la Fonque* (both Columbia).
DELFEAYO MARSALIS—*Pontius Pilate's Decision* (Novus).
ELLIS MARSALIS—*Ellis Marsalis Trio* (Blue Note).
WYNTON MARSALIS—*Wynton Marsalis, Hot House Flowers, Live at Blues Alley* (2 CDs), *The Majesty of the Blues, In This House, on This Morning* (2 CDs), *Blood on the Fields* (3 CDs) (all Columbia).

1987 Pop musician Whitney Houston becomes the first female artist to have an album go straight to number one on the *Billboard* charts.

1988 American TV evangelist Reverend Jim Bakker is forced to resign after admitting to an affair with a New York church secretary.

1996 American astronaut Shannon Lucid ends a 188-day stay in space, breaking the record of any other American or any other woman in space.

Russian jazz

The label is carefully worded, for this music, while existing under the USSR, was never Soviet in inspiration. There is also a delicious though predictable irony in that the freedom-loving U.S. of the 1980s should bring forth the conservatism of Marsalis, while the conservative USSR produces the free-ranging Ganelin Trio. Led by multi-instrumentalist Vyacheslav Ganelin (b.1944), the trio revealed that Russian jazz was not just derivative revivalism, but in certain hands mixed American free jazz and European improv. The trio and other improvising groups from as far afield as Archangel and Siberia created considerable interest in Western Europe during the 1980s for the *samizdat* nature of their work.

Branford Marsalis: at first in his brother's shadow, but now with a voice of his own.

Hot House Flowers he used an orchestra to lush effect (shades of Gil Evans here), paid tribute to his blues roots on *Majesty of the Blues*, produced on *In This House*, one of the few devotional pieces of jazz since Ellington's sacred concerts, and, even more Ellingtonian in scope, composed a history of slavery in *Blood on the Fields*. This is jazz's heritage updated and given a glossy, digitally recorded sheen, for Marsalis is vehemently opposed to the innovations of the 1960s and even more opposed to jazz rock.

Yet his reasoning is sound, for Marsalis the proselytizer for jazz is trying to make sure that jazz receives due recognition as the major African-American art form of the century. Hence the seasons of jazz hosted in New York's Lincoln Center, the black tie and tux, the reverence for the past. But his mission requires talent to bring it off, and that quality Marsalis possesses to excess. His tone is bell-like in its clarity, he is equally adept in all registers and at all speeds, and his articulation and control are superb. In that most demanding of settings, the live performance in a small club, his performance at the Blues Alley in Washington, D.C., left no one in any doubt. As his brother Branford said, "Wynton is good for jazz. End of conversation."

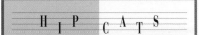

H I P   C A T S

Ellis Marsalis *(b.1934) is a pianist of distinction, adept at surprising interpretations of standards. Oldest son* **Branford** *(b.1960) plays tenor and soprano sax, firmly in the tradition at first, but, more hip than Wynton, moving toward rap music by the time of* Buckshot la Fonque. *Trombonist* **Delfeayo** *(b.1965) has also produced albums for Branford, while drummer* **Jason** *(b.1977) is on his way.*

1984 Apple launches the first Macintosh (the "Mac")—the user-friendly computer.

1986 British pop star Boy George is convicted of possessing heroin.

1988 The antidepressant drug Prozac is launched.

1984~present

Off the Streets
M-Base

The last fifteen years or so have been an incoherent period in jazz history, with numerous styles clamoring for attention and ascendancy. Marsalis walked the heritage trail, Murray et al. exploited recently gained freedoms, while Zorn and his postmodern pranksters rampaged around the detritus of modern culture. For the average poor kid in Brooklyn or other urban nightmares, none of these styles held any particular attraction.

Steve Coleman: struggling with the problem of reconciling the music of the streets with his own considerable jazz improvisatory skills.

Taking the black street music of rap, hip-hop, and funk and allying them to jazz was never going to be easy, but alto saxophonist *Steve COLEMAN* (b.1956) tried. With his band Five Elements—the name comes from a kung-fu movie—Coleman attempted "a certain balance of structure and improvisation which will express our lives and time," or M-Base—Macro-Basic Array of Structured Extemporization. The M-Base team, including saxophonists *Greg OSBY* (b.1960), *Gary THOMAS* (b.1961), and others, almost all recording for JMT, produced streetwise music in which the dominance of melody was replaced by the shifting rhythms of funk. Good in intent,

much of the music was too clever in production and suffered for its tricky structures and complex themes. But M-Base served as an excellent finishing school, with many of its musicians flourishing in different locations—Coleman with bassist Dave Holland, Osby in a more refined, contemplative mood on Blue Note records.

Out of that finishing school came two remarkable women. Pianist *Geri ALLEN* (b.1957) started out with M-Base but is far too wide-ranging a performer to be so restricted in style. Her trio albums with Haden and Motian are outstanding for her ability to play quietly and with humor. She

1994 Former Arkansas state employee Paula Jones files a suit for sexual harassment against President Bill Clinton.

1996 French woman Jeanne Calment celebrates her 121st birthday with the release of *The March of Time*, a record album of rap and techno beats.

1997 Timothy Leary, writer, former Harvard professor, and advocate of psychedelics and LSD, who coined the phrase "tune in, turn on and drop out," becomes the first person to have launched into orbit.

tackles a range of standards and less well-known songs from the repertoire, but throughout there is a sense of restrained fire that occasionally scorches. Also adept at tackling standards is singer *Cassandra WILSON* (b.1955), whose first albums with JMT were unfocused compromises between

---

ALL THAT JAZZ

GERI ALLEN—*Live at the Village Vanguard* (DIW) —a trio set with Charlie Haden and Paul Motian.

DJANGO BATES—*Winter Truce* (JMT).

STEVE COLEMAN—*Motherland Pulse, Five Elements* (both JMT); *The Tao of Mad Phat/Fringe Zones* (Novus).

JULIAN JOSEPH—*In Concert at Wigmore Hall* (East West)—live with special guests.

GREG OSBY—*Mindgames, Black Book* (both Blue Note).

COURTNEY PINE—*Journey to the Urge Within* (Island) ; *Modern Day Jazz Stories* (Antilles)—a fascinating fusion of many of Pine's musical interests.

ANDY SHEPPARD—*Soft on the Inside* (Antilles)— stellar big band session.

GARY THOMAS—*Seventh Quadrant* (JMT).

CASSANDRA WILSON—*Blues Skies* (JMT); *Blue Light 'Til Dawn, New Moon Daughter* (both Blue Note).

Courtney Pine: British new wave.

M-Base funk and jazz vocalizing. Her shift to Blue Note elevated her to the front rank of jazz interpreters, with a nice line in off-beat cover songs— Robert Johnson blues classics, the Monkees' *Last Train to Clarksville*, U2's *Love Is Blindness*—and a better line on her own compositions, most notably the luminous *Solomon Sang* on *New Moon Daughter*. With a hauntingly deep, limpid voice, she commands instant attention to every word she sings. Quite, quite glorious.

Cassandra Wilson: liquid gold voice.

British Jazz

During the 1980s British jazz enjoyed something of a resurgence. Not a revival, since Britain has always had an active jazz scene and some world-class if overlooked performers, but an upsurge from two distinct sources. One was centered around a group of largely black musicians, notably saxophonist Courtney Pine (b.1964) and pianist Julian Joseph (b.1967), who drew on the full range of black musics—soul, reggae, and African as well as jazz—and attracted a vast, previously jazz-free audience drawn as much to their sharp style as to their music. The other source was largely white and grew out of the Loose Tubes rehearsal big band. Theirs was a more "English" sound— quirky, folk-influenced, rural rather than urban, slightly blokish—which hasn't quite worked out which way to go next. Meanwhile saxophonist Andy Sheppard (b.1957) and others who have been around the block a few times gained from all the hype while continuing to develop their own take on modern jazz.

2000 Everything comes to a standstill as people pause to celebrate the year 2000; and it's back to basics as the world feels the effects of the millennium bug.

2012 President Bill Gates introduces the first Internet concert to be broadcast live. The Rolling Stones get together for the occasion to celebrate 50 years in showbiz.

2019 The first cross-channel bridge opens, stretching from Ramsgate to Calais.

????
Now–Future
The Shape of Jazz to Come?

The future of jazz: club-shaped for a new generation of dancers, just like it was in the 1930s?

As jazz gets stuck into its second century, it is hard to picture how it will progress in the next decade, let alone the entire century. So rather than go waffling on about the impact of electronics, or techno or dance music, or drum and bass, or world globalization, or the Internet—there is already a Kind of Blue *Web site from which you download a control program and insert your CD into the CD-ROM drive—let's take a selection of albums released in the last few years and plot what they suggest.*

Lots of jazz themes and riffs have already been sampled by producers and musicians, notably in hip hop and rap, and entire songs have been reworked—Herbie Hancock's *Cantaloupe Island* is particularly favored. But *Panthalassa* is unique. Producer Bill Laswell has taken a batch of Miles Davis tunes from 1969–74—when Teo Macero spent days in the studio creating albums out of the hours of music recorded—and reconstructed and remixed them. It is still Miles's music, but Macero's constructions have

ALL THAT JAZZ

DON BYRON—*Plays the Music of Mickey Katz, Bug Music* (both Elektra Nonesuch).
MILES DAVIS—*Panthalassa* (Columbia).
SCOTT HAMILTON—*East of the Sun* (Concord).
JOE HENDERSON—*The State of the Tenor* (Blue Note, 2 CDs).
JOE MANERI QUARTET—*Dahabenzapple* (hat ART).
NILS PETTER MOLVÆR—*Khmer* (ECM).
JOHN SURMAN—*Thimar* (ECM).
KENNY WHEELER—*Angel Song* (ECM).

Joe Henderson, breathing new life into bop.

2025 Grand old man of the movies, Macaulay Culkin comes out of retirement to make a cameo appearance in the first 3-D interactive film, a remake of the 1990s classic *Titanic*.

2028 Lancastrian clog dancing becomes the latest dance craze to sweep across America.

2035 King William V of Britain pays a visit to the moon to attend the opening of the first lunar vacation complex.

been replaced by Laswell's. Is this the shape of jazz to come—a new century's makeover on last century's music, a process in which recording studios hum with activity but no musicians are present?

Or is the shape of jazz to come—SOJTC—trumpeter Nils Petter Molvær's *Khmer*, using samples—one of them from a Bill Laswell-produced set (how incestuous this all is)—within washes of electronically

The future of jazz: world-melting-pot-shaped, raiding everyone else's tradition to prop up its own?

enhanced sound. Or is it the collaboration of John Surman with Tunisian oud player Anouar Brahem, the latest in a long line of Western jazz meets (anybody and everybody from all parts of the globe) and tries to come to some sort of accommodation. As (if?) jazz runs out of tunes, does it turn elsewhere for ideas?

The SOJTC could also be microtonal, as in the hands of Joe Maneri, using the notes between the notes to create a music closer to serialism than the blues. It could also be the postmodern archaeology of clarinetist Don Byron's tributes to klezmer bandleader Mickey Katz and cartoon music composer Raymond Scott, and could certainly be angry—Byron has remarked that "jazz is a curse that works to keep black musicians in their place. I especially don't like the term avant-garde—it's the 'N' word of jazz." Or it could be what it always has been—classic small-group acoustic jazz with well-crafted solos and strong themes, as in Kenny Wheeler's utterly modern and completely timeless *Angel Song*? I make no predictions.

The continuing tradition

Scott Hamilton: the mainstream personified.

Or, the SOJTC could just be what's been around for years, only more of it. Scott Hamilton (b.1954) is a tenor saxophonist remarkable for playing a music now two generations old, skipping the great saxophonists of the bop and modal eras and reverting to the swing stars of the 1930s and '40s—Lester Young, Coleman Hawkins, Johnny Hodges, *et al*. Mainstream is sometimes a derogatory term in jazz, but Hamilton's take on mainstream jazz standards is compellingly fresh. Joe Henderson (b.1937) is of an older generation than Hamilton and a staple of the Blue Note bop school, but his inspiration is the music of his boppish youth. His résumé of the state of the tenor sax in 1985 showed just how much mileage there still is in bop—to paraphrase Sonny Rollins, many of the bop pioneers had been too impatient, impoverished, beleaguered, or plain strung-out to explore every element and nuance of bop, leaving plenty of room for the likes of Henderson, and indeed Marsalis, to continue the traditions of jazz. Let's do the time warp one more time?

Jazz Speak

A selection of words that crop up in the text. You can listen to the music without them, of course, but sprinkling a few into casual conversation might impress the musically ignorant.

ACOUSTIC JAZZ—Jazz that has not been electronically enhanced in any way, although the sounds may be lightly amplified to increase their volume. Acoustic differentiates an instrument from its electric version.

ARCO—Technique of playing the double bass or other stringed instrument with a bow.

BAR—The basic metrical grouping of beats: musicians talk of playing three or whatever beats to the bar.

BEAT—A unit of measurement of rhythmic pulse. When beats are arranged in a bar, one or more of them is accented or emphasized.

BLUE NOTES—The flattening of the third, fifth, or seventh note of the major scale for expressive effect, characteristic of jazz and blues.

BLUES—A traditional African-American music, which predates jazz but has interacted with it. A blues is also a 12-bar chorus structure—when jazz musicians say "let's play the blues," they are referring to a 12-bar structure, not a style of music. Although often said, 16- and 32-bar blues are not blues at all!

BOOGIE WOOGIE—Piano style popular in the 1920s and again in the 1940s, characterized by a steady eight-note figure played repeatedly by the left hand overlaid by the right-hand melody.

BOP—Or be-bop, a revolutionary form of jazz developed during the 1940s in which solo improvisation is based on advanced harmonic changes.

CHANGES—The harmonic progression of successive chords on which jazz improvisation is based. Changes implies the specific sequence of different chords that make up a particular piece of music.

CHORD—The simultaneous playing of at least three different notes to create a single harmony. An arpeggio is the playing of the notes in ascending or descending order. Chords are the basis of harmony.

CHORUS—A single statement of the changes on which the piece is based. A solo on those changes is often many choruses in length. Confusingly, there are no verses in jazz, other than in songs.

CIRCULAR BREATHING—Breathing in through the nose while blowing out into the mouthpiece of a wind instrument to create an unbroken column of air and a sequence of notes unbroken by any breathing spaces.

COOL JAZZ—A 1950s reaction to bop, which placed more emphasis on composition than improvisation and is characterized by emotional restraint and subdued performance. Associated with the West Coast.

COUNTERPOINT—The simultaneous combination of two or more melodic lines that are related to but different from each other.

DIXIELAND—Early New Orleans jazz as performed by white musicians.

FREE JAZZ—Developed in the late 1950s, free jazz abandoned conventional rhythmic, harmonic, and melodic structures in pursuit of greater personal freedom of expression.

FUNK—A blues-influenced reaction against cool music in the 1950s, using powerful rhythms and earthy themes. Funk in jazz terms predates the entirely different funk of soul music by some years.

FUSION—A mix of two or more musics, as in jazz-rock.

GIG—A live jazz performance.

HARD BOP—The development of bop in the 1950s, more soulful and blues-influenced than original bop.

HARMONY—The simultaneous sounding of notes musically related to each other, usually in the same scale or mode; one of the main constituents of jazz music along with rhythm and melody.

IMPROV—A form of improvised music not reliant solely on jazz for its inspiration.

IMPROVISATION—The development, without premeditation, of a melody, which might be entirely spontaneous or derived from the melody, harmony, or rhythm of an existing piece of music. A short solo or an entire piece can be improvised: spontaneity is what counts.

LEGATO—Smooth; opposite of staccato, which is broken up.

MAINSTREAM—Classic, middle-of-the-road acoustic jazz from the 1930s to the present day, initially excluding such innovative styles as bop, free, and modal as they first appear but making concessions to innovation as time moves on.

MODAL—A music developed in the late 1950s in which improvisation is on a series of scales or modes rather than chords; the modes can be the familiar scales of Western music or more esoteric or historical modes.

MODERNIST—Used in the last 30 years or so to define those musicians who are alive to all forms of modern jazz; forward- rather than backward-looking.

PITCH—The location of a note, i.e., high or low.

PIZZICATO—Technique of plucking the double bass or other stringed instrument with the fingers.

POLYRHYTHM—Two or more conflicting rhythms played together.

RAGTIME—A syncopated or "ragged-time" music that predates jazz.

RHYTHM—The organization of music into strong, weak, long, and short beats. Rhythm is one of the most distinctive features of jazz.

RIFF—A short, catchy melodic or rhythmic phrase, repeated several times.

SCALE—The arrangement of a group of notes in ascending or descending order.

SCAT—A way of singing using instrumental-style vocal improvisation.

SOUL JAZZ—A development of hard bop in the 1950s with roots in gospel music.

STANDARDS—Popular songs, many from musicals, used as a basis for jazz improvisation.

STRIDE—Piano style of the 1930s named after the striding motion of the pianist's left hand.

SWING—The tension between the regular beat and the emphases placed by musicians ahead of or behind that beat. Swing music developed in the 1920s and 1930s, but overall jazz has swing in a way that classical music does not.

TIMBRE—The tone or color of an instrumental or vocal sound.

TRADITIONAL JAZZ—Originally used to define and distinguish New Orleans jazz from swing, Trad jazz was later used to describe the revival of New Orleans and Dixieland jazz in the 1940s and its imitations in Britain in the late 1950s.

VIBRATO—The creation of a rich tone color by giving a note a rapid but slight fluctuation of pitch.

Jazz Record Labels

You shouldn't gauge the quality of a jazz record solely from its label, but labels—in jazz as in fashion—are good indicators of content, quality, and hype, as well as giving the artist a certain cachet. So for the fashion-conscious jazz fan, here are 20 labels to own with pride. One word of warning: many small independent labels have been subsumed within corporate logos, so be prepared to be confused.

ATLANTIC—Founded in New York in 1947 by Ahmet Ertegun. Together with his brother Nesuhi and Jerry Wexler, these three brought the label considerable commercial success. Huge roster including R&B stars like Ray Charles, mainstream jazz (notably MJQ), '60s soul with Aretha Franklin, and, most crucially, the '60s avant-garde, notably Coltrane and Coleman.

BLACK SAINT and SOUL NOTE—Two sister Italian labels, formed in Milan in the late 1970s, which recorded more of New York's finest than any American label. David Murray, Billy Bang, Bill Dixon, and for a time Andrew Hill all appeared with their names on the orange and rainbow-colored record spines.

BLUE NOTE—Most prestigious of jazz labels, formed in 1939 by Alfred Lion. Began with boogie woogie and trad jazz, it blossomed after the war as the home of hard bop, soul jazz, and '60s superstars, notably Hancock and Shorter. Reappeared in the 1980s with a patchy roster, but still capable of top-flight jazz. Engineer Rudy van Gelder and his recording studio at Englewood Cliffs, New Jersey, are joint guarantees of quality. Cover artwork always stylish. Now part of EMI.

COLUMBIA (CBS, SONY)—Corporate giant, and home to Miles Davis, jazz-rock, Marsalis, and the new traditionalists, and also many 1940s big bands.

CONCORD—Formed in California in 1973, Concord specializes in swing and bop music and in mainstream musicians like Scott Hamilton.

CONTEMPORARY—Founded by Lester Koenig in Los Angeles in 1951, Contemporary was one of the main outlets of West Coast jazz, which is how it came to record Ornette Coleman's first sessions. Now part of Fantasy Records.

DIAL—Ross Russell's label, formed in Hollywood in 1946, recorded some of Charlie Parker's finest music. Now available through Spotlite Records.

DIW—Japanese label responsible for many modernists, including David Murray, James "Blood" Ulmer, and the Art Ensemble.

ECM—Manfred Eicher's 1969 creation in Cologne, Germany, has been responsible for defining the sound of modern European jazz— cool, clean, sometimes clinical, but always essential. With more than 650 recordings and a parallel New Series of contemporary music to its credit, ECM has brought us Jarrett, Surman, Garbarek, and more.

ESP—Home of Esperanto and the New Things of 1960s jazz, including Albert Ayler.

GRP—Grusin–Rosen Productions, epitome of easy listening jazz-rock fusion and now part of MCA. Derided by critics, loved by fans.

HAT ART—With hatOLOGY, hat Musics, and others, the home of free and experimental jazz.

IMPULSE—Formed in 1960 as a subsidiary of ABC-Paramount, Impulse built up a huge catalog of modern and cutting-edge jazz, including John Coltrane and Duke Ellington.

INCUS—London-based label formed in 1970 by Derek Bailey, Tony Oxley, and Evan Parker; still producing improv and free jazz.

PABLO—Formed in 1973 by Norman Granz and named after Picasso, this is one of the major mainstream jazz labels with a fine roster of stars including Ella Fitzgerald and Oscar Peterson.

PACIFIC JAZZ—This West Coast jazz label extended its scope in 1958 as the first American label to record Ravi Shankar. Best known for its Mulligan Baker quartet releases.

PRESTIGE—Home in the 1950s to Miles Davis, John Coltrane, and Thelonious Monk, Prestige became chiefly associated with soul jazz in the 1960s.

RIVERSIDE—Founded in 1953 to reissue classic jazz recordings, it soon established itself, alongside Prestige and Blue Note, as one of the best jazz labels of the 1950s, recording some of Bill Evans's finest work. Riverside and Prestige are now part of Fantasy and reissued under the Milestones and Original Jazz Classics (OJC) labels.

VERVE—Formed by Norman Granz in 1956 and home to *Ella's Songbooks*, the label finished up as part of the Polygram empire and is once again a major label for contemporary and reissued jazz.

Where to listen

Numerous pubs and bars have live jazz bands, and most cities have specialized jazz clubs, but if you want to indulge yourself, it's festivals you're after. Don't be put off—less muddy than Glastonbury and not quite as historic as Woodstock, with better restrooms and nicer food, jazz festivals are like opera festivals, just as civilized but much more fun. Every major city in the U.S. and Europe now has its own festival, so tourist potential features as much as the jazz on offer.

ANTIBES/JUAN LES PINS, *France (July)*—Headliners and great support acts drawn from all jazz generations and performing next to the Mediterranean.

BRECON, *Wales (August)*—Mainly mainstream acts with the occasional surprise packed into a small market town.

CORK, *Ireland (October)*—Sponsored by Guinness, which is fine by most jazz fans. Everything from early jazz to bop and beyond.

ESTORIL, *Portugal (July)*—Small and perfectly formed modern jazz festival held outside Lisbon.

MONTREUX, *Switzerland (July)*—Famous for its television broadcasts and lakeside venue, Montreux is strong on jazz-funk, a little light on pure jazz.

NEW ORLEANS, *LA (April–May)*—A jazz and heritage festival celebrating the best of New Orleans and the rest of jazz and blues.

NEWPORT, *RI (August)*—Historic festival now much reduced in size.

NEW YORK, *NY (June)*—Big enough to have its own fringe festival organized by the Knitting Factory; both are star-studded enough to break the bank.

NICE, *France (July)*—Held annually since 1948, the granddaddy of European festivals is now increasingly given over to rock and jazz-funk.

NORTH SEA, *The Hague, Netherlands (July)*—A vast, sprawling affair, mixing everything from headlining funk bands to the wildest shores of free jazz. Something for everyone for three solid days.

SAMOIS-SUR-SEINE, *France (June)*—Annual festival of Djangology.

UMBRIA, *Italy (July)*—Multivenued regional festival offering swing to jazz-rock.

Index